Gifted Children at Home

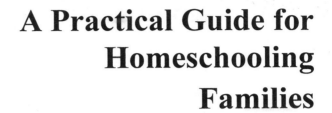

A Practical Guide for Homeschooling Families

- Characteristics

- Testing

- Curriculum

- Resources

- ... and much more!

by Janice Baker
Kathleen Julicher
Maggie S. Hogan

Cover Design:
   Christy Shaffer

Copy Editor:
   Sherri Valenzuela

Gifted Children at Home

◆ ━━━━━━━━━━━━━ ◆

A Practical Guide for Homeschooling Families

ISBN: 1-892427-01-X
Library of Congress Catalog Card Number: 2001087780

Scripture taken from the HOLY BIBLE, NEW INTERNATIONAL VERSION. Copyright 1973, 1978, 1984 International Bible Society. Used by permission of Zondervan Bible Publishers.

Designed and Published in the United States of America by:
The Gifted Group Publishing
PO Box 333
Cheswold, DE 19936
(877) 492-8081

Acknowledgments

Many thanks to the group of gifted homeschooled kids and their moms who took the time to fill out our surveys and thoughtfully answer our questions! Your honesty in sharing your joys and concerns has certainly enriched our work. Thank you all.

Charlie Baker - Thanks for your consistent encouragement and support. You keep me going!

Mark Julicher - For your friendship all these years, your faithfulness to your family, and your patient proofreading. Thank you!

Bob Hogan - This never would have happened without you; thanks for being my cheering section.

And to our kids:
Seth Baker
Lauren Baker
Megan Baker
Joseph Julicher
Esther Julicher
Daniel Julicher
Sarah Julicher
J.B. Hogan
Tyler Hogan
...if it weren't for you guys we wouldn't have needed to write this book! We love you very much

James 1:17 "Every good and perfect gift is from above, coming down from the Father of the heavenly lights, who does not change like shifting shadows."

Table of Contents

Introduction
The Big Picture

Gift **- "Something good, often given undeservedly or unexpectedly."**

"Education is not the filling of a pail, but the lighting of of a fire."
- William Butler Yeats

We're not experts in the field of giftedness. Although we have various degrees between us, none are in the area of giftedness issues. What we know we have learned through 'OJT,' on the job training. We're simply three Christian moms who have chosen to home educate our intellectually gifted children and have spent countless hours seeking out the very best possible education for our kids. Through our homeschooling education, we have learned so much about giftedness and homeschooling - from our successes and our failures - that we wanted to share this information with others. The information in this book is a tool you can use for guiding your decisions about educating your children.

At first we felt somewhat isolated in our experiences, thinking there were few parents struggling with this issue. When we began offering a workshop on homeschooling gifted kids we discovered very quickly that there's an army of us out there!

Every place we went we experienced the same scenario. Conference Leader: "We'd like you to do your workshop, but of course it will be a very small group attending." If three or four people were expected, twelve showed up. If we had room for twenty-five, forty would come. When over one hundred crammed the aisles and doorways and halls in a room meant for fifty we finally caught on! We believe an entire population in the homeschool community is being dramatically under-served or even ignored because:

✍ As state and support group leaders, we've noticed a high percentage of gifted students. We've heard the same from other leaders with whom we've spoken.
✍ We've observed a high percentage in other homeschool groups.
✍ The gifted tend to be under-served in conventional schools and parents often turn to homeschooling for answers.
✍ Society wants to believe that everyone is intellectually capable of learning the same material, given enough time. (Hence outcomes-based education and lack of commitment to gifted students.)

✍ If only ten percent of the estimated one million plus homeschoolers are gifted, then there are approximately one hundred thousand gifted children being homeschooled in the United States.

✍ Parents often feel uncomfortable discussing their children's accelerated academic abilities and needs and so tend to remain quiet about it, leading to a lack of networking. (1)

✍ There are very few support groups or newsletters we're aware of dealing specifically with the homeschool gifted. See Chapter Sixteen, Resources and Notes. (2)

On a more philosophical level, treatment of gifted kids in the public school system and in society as a whole has steadily declined over the past few decades. Today, identifying the gifted isn't "politically correct." Consider the powerful indictment of gifted education from <u>How Schools are Shortchanging the Gifted</u>, by Sally M. Reis, professor and researcher with the University of Connecticut's National Research Center on the Gifted and Talented.

> "Because schools have focused for decades on lifting up the lowest achievers, they are shortchanging the brightest students. High-ability children are not challenged in most classrooms and endure a steady diet of dumbed-down textbooks, and repetition of skills that they have mastered years ago. They suffer from the elimination of many forms of advanced or accelerated classes because it has become politically incorrect to separate students on the basis of ability. Furthermore, a widely used teaching technique called cooperative learning assigns the highest achieving students to position of peer teacher - essentially pressing them into service as teacher aides." (3)

To be honest, it appears to be more acceptable today to be athletically gifted, musically gifted, artistically gifted, or even socially gifted than intellectually gifted. Even within the homeschooling community, there's a definite sense of isolation among the parents with whom we've spoken.

Homeschooling parents have reported lack of understanding in support groups. They might have a question like: "I don't know what to do about Kelly's math. She scored 97% on her achievement test but she's spending almost no time on her math studies. She's bored and not working to her ability. Is there a curriculum that would better motivate her?" Now, this is a legitimate concern, but how many people would perceive it as such? Most would think it a thinly disguised attempt at bragging, and furthermore, Kelly is obviously doing well in math, so they conclude that she doesn't need any help.

One woman made this observation about her support group meeting, "Mention that your child is ADD or dyslexic, and there's usually understanding. Mention that she's gifted and receive a cold shoulder. Why can't others realize that we need support and resources, too?" Discussing an educational problem related to your gifted child is greeted with about as much enthusiasm as saying, "I really need to gain some weight."

We need to be sensitive in looking for answers, of course. But, parents are as responsible for searching out the best in education, resources, and opportunities for their gifted learners as for their athletes, musicians, learning disabled, and physically challenged students. Just as these children require specialized approaches, so do our gifted kids. It's not enough to say, "They're so smart - they'll do fine no matter what." What about boredom? Frustration? Insufficient challenge? These students need to be encouraged, challenged, and motivated in order to grow fully into the young men and women they are capable of becoming.

We hope this book will encourage you in educating your gifted child. Our goal is to provide you with the information and resources that will enable you to do so with confidence and success. Parents of the gifted have shown up at our workshops, hungry for information. From them, we hear expressions of the same concerns we've had in homeschooling our own gifted kids. For these parents, we wrote this book.

Resources and Notes

1) We've begun handing out surveys when we speak about giftedness at conferences. You'll find comments from both children and parents scattered throughout the book. If you'd like to fill out a survey, please write us. We'd love to hear from you! (Our addresses are on page 122.)

2) You'll find "Notes and Resources" after each chapter, as well as an Appendix and a section of reproducible forms in the back.

3) Reis, Sally M. (1994). How Schools are Shortchanging The Gifted, Technology Review, April.

Chapter One
How Do I Know If My Child's Gifted?

How do I know if my child is gifted? It's a question we hear time and time again during our workshops. As well, there are other questions that usually accompany it, among them: What is giftedness? Who are the gifted and how does the term apply to us who school at home? These are some of the questions we will attempt to answer in this chapter.

At the most basic level, the word "gifted" means that this person has the ability to think or do beyond the abilities of average people. More technical definitions tell us about specific abilities. Lists of distinguishing characteristics are also beneficial in identifying giftedness. Let's go over a few of these definitions and characteristics so that we can understand gifted people and who they are.

Everyday, we see people who understand things faster, learn easier, or perform certain tasks far better than others. We say that these people have a gift for something, like a gift for languages, or a gift for music. Their minds, or their bodies, or both just seem to function very well. So first, giftedness is a handy expression used to describe outstanding ability. If that person is outstanding in a specific area, we acknowledge that ability. We say that a musician is musically gifted or that a sculptor is artistically gifted. We call a person who learns easily and thinks well or differently, intellectually gifted. This book is primarily devoted to this latter group of people, although the characteristics and qualities of giftedness also apply to others of outstanding abilities.

According to Dr. Webb, in *Guiding the Gifted Child*, a gifted person is one who scores in the top two percent of a population on a special test called an intelligence test. (1) There are many tests which tell this information, each of them slightly different, but each test uses a number to denote intelligence, the Intelligence Quotient, or IQ. The IQ is nothing more than an attempt to measure the differences in thinking we have noticed. Tests, testing, and IQ will be discussed later in this book, so for now, let's cover more about types of giftedness.

Giftedness appears to be uneven. We can observe that some children are better in math or music than they are in, say, English or sports. As there seem to be many aspects of giftedness, some experts have grouped these gifts. In *Frames of Mind: The Theory of Multiple Intelligences*, Howard Gardner advances the following as specific types of giftedness:

> Musical Intelligence
> Logical-Mathematical Intelligence
> Spatial Intelligence
> Bodily-Kinesthetic Intelligence
> Interpersonal and Intrapersonal Intelligences

He believes that there are other areas which could be listed here as types of giftedness, too, and in the future, we will probably see more types of giftedness being described in books about multiple intelligences. (2)

Traditionally, though, intellectual giftedness is the concept psychologists mean when they use the term "gifted." Although much of what we have to say is applicable to other gifts as well, this book concentrates primarily on intellectual giftedness.

When is intellectual giftedness obvious to parents? Actually, it isn't always obvious. When a first child is gifted, the parents often think that the child is normal and so the early signs go unnoticed. But, sooner or later, signs crop up. Parents may realize their child is "different," unusual, or outstanding long before he or she is of school age.

> *JB was a 9-month-old when he was given a developmental test by our pediatrician's nurse practitioner. He was sitting on my lap when she put a small alphabet block on the table in front of him. He picked it up. She then placed another down and he picked it up in his other hand. She put a third block on the table. He looked at it for a instant, and then immediately picked it up - in his mouth! She sat still, puzzled. I asked what was the matter, and she said she didn't know how to score that response, she'd never seen it before. (He was expected to either put one block down or try to put two blocks in one hand.) That was the first objective confirmation of our gut feeling that we were dealing with a "different" child. - Maggie*

Do you have a "different" child? Do you have a 9-month-old who is talking; a 4-year-old who taught herself to read; an 8-year-old who grasps concepts so quickly it takes your breath away; a 12-year-old who can recite everything you'd possibly want to know about computers; or a 15-year-old who has written an incredible short novel? Here are some general attributes that indicate giftedness. Gifted students may exhibit many, but not all, of these characteristics which were gleaned from personal experience, *Guiding the Gifted Child* (3) and The Department of Education ERIC files on giftedness from the Internet. (4)

PRESCHOOL

★ Precocious sense of humor.
★ Develops faster than average (walking, talking, potty training, etc.).
★ Puts together puzzles quickly and completes more difficult puzzles than peers.
★ Catches on quickly to concepts.
★ Repeatedly asks observant, penetrating questions.
★ Can focus intensely for lengthy periods on activities of interest.
★ Early maturity (or possibly a very late bloomer!).
★ Precocious use of language (as in puns).
★ May need little sleep.
★ May show extreme emotional sensitivity.

SCHOOL AGE

★ Often displays a highly developed sense of humor.
★ Continues to be curious about everything.
★ Many interests and hobbies - sometimes prefers to study one with intensity.
★ Is into collections.
★ Perfectionist.
★ Extremely competitive.
★ Very active imagination.
★ Different perspective on ideas, sees unusual connections and twists.
★ May be a lone worker.
★ Displays higher level thinking than peers.
★ Original thinker and doer, may be nonconformist.
★ May display leadership abilities.
★ May attempt to do math work in head.
★ Advanced vocabulary, used naturally. (Although they may not be able to pronounce words correctly they've never heard, but only read.)
★ May not do equally well in every subject.

Can your child be gifted if he or she only shows half of these characteristics? Yes, and it helps to remember that this is a list of attributes which are very commonly found in gifted children, but not in all gifted children. Certainly, most gifted children will not exhibit all of these attributes. In addition, some characteristics may be hidden and, because of a host of good reasons, may not appear until much later. (5)

While the characteristics in the list above all sound pretty good, there are also a few more difficult characteristics:
★ Perfectionism.
★ Supersensitivity, or heightened senses.
★ Very intense emotionalism.

★ High energy levels.
★ Needs little sleep (~ 25% need little sleep while ~25% need more than normal). (6)
★ Persistence (or stubbornness).
★ May start too many projects and have trouble finishing them.
★ Dislike taking time for precision.
★ May enjoy learning a new skill more than using it.
★ May be impatient with details.
★ May be concerned with morals and existence very early.
More information on characteristics of the gifted is available. (7)

These characteristics may be the most long lasting and definitely are the most frustrating. A baby who is ready for play at 5 a.m., a preschooler who must have her books in the right order, or a youngster who refuses to try to do something even though she did it yesterday can drive a mom to distraction and yet be a perfectly normal gifted child. Some of the more negative characteristics can lead parents and teachers to erroneously conclude that a child is not gifted, but learning disabled, hyperactive, or rebellious. In Chapter Four, we'll go over these qualities and see how they relate to schooling.

If your child displays many of these attributes and you believe he's gifted, he probably is. To confirm your belief you may consider having him/ or her psychologically evaluated. Whether or not you have him evaluated is a personal decision. Many parents understand that giftedness can be confirmed through testing, but still question whether it is really necessary. Our answer? It depends! We recommend yes, if you're trying to gain access to certain programs or scholarships, although some of them allow parental recommendations in lieu of test scores. We recommend no, if you have no interest in pursuing those options. And what about the results of the test? Would you treat your child differently if she tested gifted, or not? Would your expectations then seem unrealistic? Would your perceptions of her abilities color the way she sees herself? These are big questions that deserve reflection and honest answers. For more decision-making information on testing, read on.

Testing: the Evaluation of Giftedness

The history of intelligence testing is fascinating. Joel Shurkin's book, *Terman's Kids*, is well worth reading to understand the origins of the Stanford-Binet Human Intelligence Scale and the Stanford Achievement Tests. The book describes the tests, their usefulness, and their limitations. Decisions about testing are easier when you know more about the tests. (8)

If you've decided that your child should be tested, ask yourself several questions to determine the appropriate test:

- Am I looking for an IQ test?
- Am I looking for an achievement test percentile?
- Am I looking for a developmental test?
- Am I looking for a behavioral evaluation?

It's important to know why you're testing in order to choose the most effective test. Often, psychologists will use a battery of tests to provide a broader picture of your child's abilities. Intelligence testing may not be the only test results you want to see. You may want to find out if your child has any learning disabilities, or if your child is adapting well to an emotional situation. [Note: School can be a very emotional place which can influence your child's testing.] You may question if little Sally is ready for reading, or regular school work. Evaluating for these different types of information requires different tests. There are several intelligence tests, each of which tests a bit differently, as well as tests which show achievement, development, and other information you may need. A carefully chosen combination of tests provides the most accurate picture of where your child is and what she is capable of doing. Fortunately, many psychologists use a battery of tests which can be included in an efficient and affordable package. An outside evaluation is also useful if you're dealing with a problem schooling situation or as a launching point to plan your homeschool year.

The IQ test is never a measure of the value of a child, but is rather an attempt to quantify the child's intellectual abilities.

The top two percent of a population means about 125 to 130 IQ, depending upon the tests used. The normal tests given are the WISC (Revised or III) or the Stanford-Binet (IV or LM). The parentheses show the most common versions of these tests. Though the two versions of each are essentially the same type of test, they're scored very differently and will measure different things. For example, the WISC tests and the Stanford-Binet IV were developed to measure the middle part of the population, which means they cannot discriminate between the moderately gifted and the extremely gifted. To do this, the Stanford-Binet LM is recommended. (9) You may find this test helpful if your child scores well on one of the other measures of intelligence, in the top one percent, for example, or has two or more subtest scores (as in the WISC) of > 16. (10) Some other tests which can measure intelligence are the Cognitive Abilities Test, the Mensa IQ test, and the Otis-Lenin Test.

A child may score very differently on different tests. For example, a WISC score may be significantly lower than a Stanford-Binet, not only because they are different tests, but also because they don't use the same scale. In addition, some tests are administered in a written format while others are verbal. Your child may have a problem in one of these formats which has nothing to do with intelligence but which may seriously affect his score (and his schooling, by the way). It's very important to remember that these tests are merely tools we can use to provide the best assessment possible for our children.

An achievement test is different from an intelligence test. It measures learned knowledge or academic skills, whereas the intelligence test attempts to measure thinking skills like analysis, divergent thinking, or understanding of concepts. The kind of achievement test a psychologist administers will be slightly different from the Stanford Achievement test, Iowa Basic Skills Tests, or the Metropolitan Achievement test we are used to seeing. When a child scores at a sixth grade reading level on a Woodcock Johnson or a Wide Range Achievement Test, you can be sure that he is actually reading on that level. A child who scores at the 99 percentile on an achievement test yet scores in the average range on an intelligence test should probably be retested with another type of IQ test.

> *When Joseph took the Stanford-Binet, he had just gotten healthy from a severe cold and just did not "take" to the tester. When he's uncomfortable, Joe will clam up (for him, a very unusual thing as he's a talker!) and because the S-B is a verbally administered test, the implications for the accuracy of his score are obvious. Fortunately, he scored well enough for our purposes, i.e., to skip a grade. I didn't know then what I know now: that I should have asked for a reevaluation.   - Kathleen*

How can you make sure that the testing is reasonably accurate and a good experience? First, become familiar with the test. Then, have the child tested under the best of circumstances.

PREPARING THE CHILD FOR TESTING
► Explain the testing procedure
► Plan for a good night's sleep
► Eat a nutritious meal before testing
► The student should be comfortable with the tester and the test site
► The test should be a reasonable length for the child's attention span
► Encourage them to do their best, but don't overly stress performance
► Never test all day!
► Don't put off testing - test when you can use the results
► Teach them the "rules of doing mazes"

Test day: The tests, the way they are administered, and the environmental conditions during testing will have an impact on your child's score.

Some tests rely upon the idea that your child already knows how to do mazes, codes, etc. A young child may not have had the rules explained to him. For example, your child may not know they are not to touch the lines of a maze at all. One of our children didn't maximize his score because his drawings were proportionally the same, not actual size. He was told to "draw it exactly like the picture."

> *We've had several less than ideal testing situations   JB's first IQ test was done while attending a public kindergarten. Amazingly, they chose to test him on the day of the big Valentine's Party. I'm sure this 5-year-old was paying close attention to the test while imagining what he was missing out on in the way of food and games! When JB was seven, we met with a school psychologist after he'd finished testing JB, and discovered he had a very thick accent. As he went over the scores with us, he mentioned that the only place JB didn't perform in the superior range was in a timed section with patterns. Knowing JB and his ability with patterns, we were surprised. Upon questioning JB later, we learned he never understood that this particular part of the test was timed. He had decided to go slowly to make sure he got them all correct. (He did get them right, but only finished part of them.) Without any prompting from us, he said the tester was difficult to understand.*
> *- Maggie*

Obviously, test conditions play an important factor in the accuracy of test results. While there may be no perfect settings, you can do much to minimize poor conditions by being aware of different factors.

How do I interpret the results? The psychologist will help you on this and there are several books which can also explain the tests. Feel free to ask any question you can think of about the tests while you are in the debrief with the psychologist.

EXCELLENT QUESTIONS TO ASK:
⇨   What's the range of IQ tested by this test?
⇨   Does my child score at the top of the testing range for the entire test or for any of the subtests? If so, on how many of the subtests has my child scored at or near the top? Which ones were they?

⇨ What percentile is this score?

⇨ What is my child's mental age?

⇨ Were there any problem areas? What are they? (This is important for planning. A problem area for a gifted child may be indicated by an average score in a subtest.)

These questions will help you get a handle on the test results and allow you to start planning for your year.

OK, now you have a score. Is your child gifted or not? We are back to the question of the definition of gifted. According to the IQ score, it's about 130 and above. For the purposes of a school or program, there are other things to take into account before the child is considered qualified. Of course, for the purposes of homeschool, we can give our children the education of a gifted child without worrying about qualification.

What do public schools use to determine giftedness? Each state, or even each school district, has its own parameters. Often, as part of the nominating procedure (the process of asking parents and/or teachers and/or psychologists who they think belongs in the gifted program) they will ask parents to fill out a form. This form has questions on it pertaining to the types of characteristics referred to earlier. If a parent observes enough of these behaviors, they believe there's a good indication the child should be tested for giftedness. What about special programs? Entry into any program is dependent upon whom the program is designed to serve. Some use a set IQ of anywhere from 120 to 145, while others use a matrix of different factors to choose their students.

Because an achievement test will only correctly identify perhaps half of gifted students, some school districts use a score of 90 percentile on a standardized achievement test as an entry qualification into their programs. Johns Hopkins' Talent Search is open to seventh and eighth graders who have scored in the 97th, 98th, or 99th percentile in the mathematics (M), verbal (V) , or composite score categories of their most recent or next-most-recent standardized aptitude or achievement tests. (More on Johns Hopkins and other Talent Search programs later.) A student who scores well on an achievement test in several areas is considered to be academically gifted, even though he may have a lower score on another subtest.

Clearly, there is no one universal definitive score or test for the gifted, just generally accepted scores within certain ranges. And even within the gifted population there's a hierarchy. The IQ scale typically looks like this:

130+ gifted (about 2 in 100 persons).
140+ highly gifted or high-end gifted (about 1 in 260 persons).
150+ (about 1 in 2,330 persons.)
160+ profoundly gifted (about 1 in 31,560 persons). (11)

Finally, the gifted child is one with the characteristic of being able to think well, or differently than the norm, and the intelligence tests are merely attempts to measure those differences. How well the tests succeed is the subject of much discussion among the experts, so just remember that tests are limited, testers are human, and your child is more than a test score.

> *Daniel was six when he was tested for learning disabilities and intelligence as well as a host of other things in an attempt to figure out what his problem was in school. The teacher had a number of bad things to say about Daniel, not the least of which was that he was hyperactive. Well, the testing was totally negative, except for the intelligence part. He scored near the top of the test and so we found ourselves being told that Daniel's only problem was that he was highly gifted. Daniel listened to the explanation and then, taking his thumb out of his mouth, said "Well, I guess that means I'm OK after all, Mommy." - Kathleen*

For more information on giftedness, testing, and characteristics of gifted children and adults, check out the resources listed, especially those on the Internet. (12-14)

Resources & Notes

1) Webb, Dr. James, Betty Meckstroth, Stephanie Tolan (1982). *Guiding the Gifted Child*, page five.

Gifted Psychology Press
P.O. Box 5057
Scottsdale, AZ 85261
Phone: 602-954-4200
Fax: 602-954-0185
www.giftedpsychologypress.com

2) Gardner, Howard. (199_). *Frames of Mind: The Theory of Multiple Intelligences*.

3) Webb, Meckstroth, and Tolan, *Guiding the Gifted Child*, Chapter Three.

4) Department of Education E R I C Clearinghouse Digest # E476 on the Internet.
     http://www.ed.gov/databases/ERIC_Digests/ed321481.html

5) Some gifted children are slow in developing their communication skills and so are not recognized as gifted. Others have significant learning disabilities for which they are able to compensate by their giftedness. The result is that the giftedness hides the learning disabilities and the disabilities hide the giftedness. The test scores may even show a 'normal' child when what you have is far from normal. See Chapter Six for more information on gifted and learning disabled.

6) Webb, Dr. James in a speech given on November 14, 1998, Louisville, KY at the National Association for Gifted Children Conference (NAGC).

7) For more information on characteristics of gifted children: check out the ERIC Digest.
     http://www.ed.gov/databases/ERIC-Digests/

Guiding the Gifted Child, See note (1).

Gifted Development Center : See note (10). Send for materials.
     Email: gifted@gifteddevelopment.com

The Hollingworth Center for the Highly Gifted
Sharon Lind
12302 SE 237th Place
Kent, WA 98031

For information or study results about gifted adults:
     The Institute for the Study of Advanced Development
     1452 Marion Street
     Denver, CO 80218
     303-837-8378
     888-GIFTED1

8) Joel N. Shurkin, (1992). *Terman's Kids - The Ground Breaking Study of How the Gifted Grow Up*; Little, Brown, & Co.

9) Psychologist Lewis Terman, creator of the Stanford-Binet IQ Test and co-developer of the Stanford Achievement Test, found 1,500 gifted kids and began the longest running life study ever undertaken. Shurkin gained access to the files and even some of the original participants and has written a fascinating account of the study's goals, accomplishments, and flaws. He presents a great historical background for understanding some of our society's views of gifted kids. Although a brilliant man, Terman's racist, sexist beliefs biased his studies of gifted youth in ways that still impact us today. Fascinating reading.

10) The Gifted Development Center in Denver, CO. can recommend evaluators in other parts of the country. Linda Silverman is a strong proponent of using the Stanford-Binet LM to test for the highly gifted.
1452 Marion Street
Denver, CO 80218
Phone: (303) 837-8378
Fax: (303) 837-7465
Email: gifted@gifteddevelopment.com

11) Linda Silverman with Kathi Kearney in a paper in support of the Stanford-Binet LM testing: "Don't Throw Away the Old Binet." Get this from The Gifted Development Center. See note (10).

12) Webb, et al., *Guiding the Gifted Child*, page 5.

13) Gifted Education News Groups on the Internet
GIFTEDNET-L:LISTSERV@LISTSERV.CC.WM.EDU
TAG-L:LISTSERV@LISTSERV.NET
TAGFAM:LISTSERV@LISTSERV.NET
GTOT-L:MAJORDOMO@ESKIMO.COM

14) Websites:
www.gifted.org
www.nagc.org
www.cec.sped.org

15) Useful Resource:
ERIC Clearinghouse on Disabilities and Gifted Education
At The Council for Exceptional Children
1110 N. Glebe Road
Arlington, VA 22201-5704
(800) 328-0272
E-mail: ericec@cec.sped.org
www.ericec.org

Advice:

Let the student work at their own pace; have plenty of resources available.
- Matthew Matheson, age 11

Don't give your kids too many breaks!
- Jessi Smith, age 7

Give them breaks when they want them, and do not give them a lot of homework.
- Laura Reisinger, age 10

Be careful to remember that even when you're a teacher, you're still a mom.
- Megan Baker, age 11

Make sure the kids have fun learning and do lots of hands-on activities.
- Tyler Hogan, age 9

I would not trade schooling Ryan for anything in the world. It is rewarding to be the one to see him learn and grow. He would be bored in a traditional classroom - this way he can be sufficiently challenged.
- Susan, mother of Ryan, age 6

Chapter Two
Should You Homeschool Your Gifted Child?

"One could get a first-class education from a shelf of books five feet long."

-Charles W. Eliot (when President of Harvard University)

Giftedness is a gift, a blessing from the One who created us. Even though it's often a challenge, let's rise to that challenge with the realization that God specifically placed this child in your care. Who better than you to raise, nurture, love, and yes, educate that child, than you? No teacher, no gifted program, no school can replace what you have been given - the right and the responsibility of raising and educating your child. You know and love them in a way others can never duplicate.

The bottom line is this: your gifted child doesn't fit into a normal classroom, primarily because he or she is not a normal child. Gifted children are quite normal in themselves, and are as they should be, but they just do not fit as a "normal" student in a classroom designed for the norm.

Some gifted children are in a group which can be called the optimally gifted. These children are gifted enough to do well, are emotionally close to normal, and 'fit in' well enough to be happy. Many others do not fit in because they're too bright, too sensitive, or simply not accepted. These children may be called the not-so-optimally gifted. Sometimes their jokes aren't laughed at, sometimes they're the objects of ridicule, and sometimes they're just plain bored. Another set of gifted children, many of them girls, fit into the social scene at school very well - so well that they turn off learning and become young persons who have suppressed their own selves in order to become accepted by peers.(1) Many deliberately make errors in order to keep from getting a good grade. Any of these children, optimal or not-so-optimal, are wonderful candidates for coming home to school. Why is this? What is it about homeschooling which is so good for gifted children? Let's go over a few reasons to homeschool.

REASONS TO HOMESCHOOL

☐ A homeschooled student has time to grow up at his or her own rate.

☐ A homeschooled child can learn at his or her own rate whether slow, fast, or changing.

☐ A homeschooled child has time for dreaming, for reading, for enjoying investigating things.

☐ A homeschooled child is free to be a child and still progress at a challenging pace.

☐ A homeschooled child bonds with his family and establishes a relationship which is difficult to break later on and which will provide loving support for the rest of his life.

☐ A homeschooled child lives with people who will take time to talk with him, laugh at his jokes, and enjoy his interests.

☐ A homeschooled child can investigate things she is interested in, like horses, or airplanes, or Legos™.

☐ A homeschooled child has less pressure to conform or to perform.

These are very strong reasons to homeschool, but how is it all done? Here are some specific questions we've been asked in seminars.

In what ways is schooling a gifted child different from schooling a non-gifted one?
Homeschooling itself is not much different. You would always want your child to learn at his or her own best rate, so you would adjust the course work to his or her needs. The same is true for a gifted child. The only difference is the size of the adjustments, the type of adjustments, and the rate at which he proceeds through the curriculum. These are the things that make a truly individualized curriculum. (2)

How do you choose curriculum for a gifted child? How do you adapt for differences?
You choose the curriculum based upon challenges offered and ease of use. Your child may need a history book which has a higher reading level and tells about important overarching ideas. If your child is a good reader, skip the readers, and probably the literature books, choosing the literature itself. In math, you can choose to skip the manipulatives when she catches on to the concept. (More detail on this in Chapter Eight.)

How do you teach what you're not "qualified" to teach?
Of all the frightening things about accepting responsibility for the education of a gifted child the biggest is "The Wall": the place beyond which you do not wish to go either by interest or by knowledge. Everyone who homeschools has a Wall but you must not be afraid of it.

But wait, you say, "What about calculus? What about Latin and logic?" True, not every parent wants to take on the task of teaching every single subject. But think about this - does home educating your child require that **you** do all the teaching? We don't believe it does. We see ourselves, especially in the upper grades, as much "facilitators" as teachers.

Practically speaking, this means that no you don't have to teach every course because perhaps one, you're not good at them and two, you don't like them, and three, you don't want to! What do you do instead? Get creative. All seasoned homeschoolers know the concept of "flexibility." Here are a number of options, we've successfully used many of them:

YOUR GIFTED CHILD CAN TAKE A COURSE BY...

✦ Barter - I'll teach your kids science if you'll teach mine math.
✦ Independent Study - there are times when kids do just fine with a textbook, individual study, and someone with them to help as needed.
✦ Tutor - we've paid a college student to be a one-on-one weekly tutor when independent study dragged. This worked very well.
✦ Computer - we've participated in a cutting edge interactive computer course called Distance Learning Project by Stanford University. This is a good option, although quite expensive. (3)
✦ Computer-based full curriculum programs. There are many on the market now.
✦ Internet. (4)
✦ Correspondence Courses. See Appendix A.
✦ Co-ops, sharing the teaching with other parents.
✦ Video.
✦ College - many students have been able to take college math and other courses during their high school and even junior high school years. Generally, colleges and universities only need a parent's signature in order to enroll a young student.

> *Seth began taking college math at age twelve and, being the bright and competitive homeschooled kid that he was, he quickly became the top student in the class. (In fact, they were soon asking him to tutor other college students.) This situation worked out very nicely for us. Seth had no problem with being the youngest because math class is not a particularly social class, and I picked him up directly after class. His college class counted for high school credit and I no longer had to worry about staying one step ahead of him in the book. - Janice*

This is a short list; it could be lengthened with a bit of brainstorming.

There are many ways around teaching classes one doesn't wish to teach, and these options are not only just as good as traditional options, some are vastly superior. That dispels the "What about calculus?" myth we so often hear.

How do you homeschool several children?
As children get older, you can consolidate subjects so that they all study topics at the same time. For example, everyone in the group may study biology together, each child using ability appropriate materials. Also, as they get older they will be able to do more independent work, releasing you to work with younger children.

Is he missing things by not being in the gifted program at school?
Now let's wander into the murky and sometimes controversial area of Gifted Program territory. (This is in reference to yearlong programs in public or private schools, not onetime special events, camps, etc.)

"My child is in the Gifted Program." It's said with a bit of pride, mixed with awe and wonder and, naturally, humility, because others officially recognize their little Georgie is a genius. Have you ever heard that? Said it? Wished it?

> *I can't poke too much fun because I've worn those shoes. I bought into the prestige and advancement that seemed to come with this honor. Because of that, I can write honestly about our disappointing experiences with public school gifted programs. Since speaking about this, I've discovered many others have been equally disappointed in their gifted programs. - Maggie*

Obviously, we've not researched every gifted program in the country. But we've seen enough to convince us that gifted programs aren't always what they appear to be. (5)

Consider these aspects of gifted programs in regular schools:

▶▶ Children in special classes know why they're there and may act as if they're superior to everyone else. These classes can be a breeding ground for ferocious egos in both children and parents - not a character trait we prefer to develop.

▶▶ Gifted classes that are "pull-out" classes force children to miss out and/or make up time missed. For example, they may miss out one day a week or one hour a day and be expected to keep up with regular work. *One program our oldest was in required him to miss recess and part of lunch-almost the only part of school he liked! - Maggie*

▶▶ Programs that are self-contained or magnet programs isolate gifted kids from "regular" kids, and often result in gifted kids being dubbed "geeks" and much worse.

▶▶ We've witnessed and heard of many New Age techniques being used in gifted programs. Don't underestimate their danger on impressionable minds. Lots of mother earth worship, visualization techniques, and an emphasis on humanism. Some are subtle; some are downright blatant.

▶▶ Lack of good solid basics in favor of the educational fad of the moment. One magnet gifted program in our area spent the entire school year studying just a make-believe society for social studies. Math or language arts can be overly emphasized or overlooked, depending on the strengths and weaknesses of the teacher. For whatever reason, gifted programs seem to be able to use almost anything as curriculum, no matter how educationally sound it is, or isn't.

▶▶ In a regular school, your gifted child may not even be admitted into a gifted program. Some of the programs have a cutoff line at 145 IQ (which is near the top of the scale of the most commonly administered tests), while others use 125 IQ plus a host of other criteria, some of which your child may not meet. Because schools usually have limited facilities for gifted programming and because the programs can be very popular with parents, they often feel they must be fairly rigid in their selection criteria.

▶▶ Selection to the gifted program may not reduce your parental problems, because then there are psychosocial problems which can crop up. For some schools, to be admitted into such a program is equivalent to being cast out into the social wilderness, especially for girls.

▶▶ Some gifted programs are really designed to stretch the normal student and use a "revolving door" entry/exit where kids choose to participate or not. Although the programs can be wonderful and a great learning experience, they may not meet the needs of an exceptionally gifted child.

▶▶ If your child is in elementary school, he may be allowed to leave class once or twice a week to attend a special class where he will learn how to use the library to do research, how to make a video tape or something else, or all about dinosaurs. This is usually called an "enrichment program" because it adds enriching experiences to the normal classroom. Children enjoy these classes unless sessions are scheduled during PE or music class, which has been known to happen.

▸▸ It may be that acceleration is the only solution to certain problems for your bright youngster. (Refer to Chapter Ten for a definition of types of acceleration.) In a school situation, the social problems associated with acceleration can seem overwhelming. Your child may be faced with choosing between an intellectually boring year or one filled with confusing emotional and relationship problems with children who are much older. An additional challenge: acceleration of one year may not be enough. In this case, social problems may be diminished since the age difference is greater. However, the acceleration dilemma may not be as difficult as it first appears. The evidence in research is clear that acceleration is of benefit in spite of the age differences, and that gifted children seem to relate well with older children in the new class. (6)

▸▸ Another type of program commonly found in regular schools is in the affective domain (feelings instead of the cognitive or academic), wherein students are counseled and led through a series of emotional experiences meant to cause children to think, reflect upon values, and evaluate the value systems of others. Many of these types of programs are administered more quietly because of their potential for upsetting parents.

▸▸ At the high school level, many schools provide their gifted students opportunities to work with their age-mates in quasi-counseling roles or in tutoring. Some of the counseling situations reported to us have concerned premarital sex, abortions, and homosexual relationships. The disturbing trend of these programs is the requirement that the gifted child not tell the parents everything. Secrecy is important, because parents throughout the country have protested them.

Parents should investigate very carefully before enrolling a child in gifted programs. Don't be lured in by the glamour and honor of being "one of the chosen." Look closely, interview thoroughly, inspect the curriculum. Homeschooling a gifted child is a challenge which requires your full attention, time, and a bit of money, but the return is much greater than the cost. Your child will be able to have freedom to study, freedom to grow and mature at his own rate, freedom from peer pressure, the full benefits of a private tutor, and appropriate curriculum. You will have freedom from pressure cooker meetings with teachers, principals, and counselors. You will never have to wonder what will happen in middle school, or high school, or on the bus. And, an added blessing, you will have your child back again without all of the sensitivities and fears school has taught him. Our families are grateful to God who has made it possible for us to homeschool!

Resources & Notes

1) Kerr, Dr. Barbara, (1997). *Smart Girls (Revised Edition): A New Psychology of Girls, Women, and Giftedness.*
> Gifted Psychology Press, Inc.: P.O. Box 5057
> Scottsdale, AZ 85261
> Phone: (602) 954-4200

Pipher, Dr. Mary, (1994). *Reviving Ophelia: Saving the Selves of Adolescent Girls*, Ballantine Books, a division of Random House.

2) Delisle, Dr. James R. (1987). *Gifted Kids Speak Out*, Free Spirit Publications. Delisle surveyed 6,000 gifted school children ages 6-13. Hundreds tell us what it means to be gifted. One comment: "Being gifted means having to stay in for kindergarten recess to do first grade math."

3) Distance Learning Project - students have the opportunity to work independently at their own pace, and to move into AP and university level math courses before leaving high school. Multimedia format. These courses are designed for self-motivated students comfortable using a computer. Tutors, who are specialists, provide feedback based on weekly reports filed electronically by their students. Textbook assignments, and assessment, help assure on-going mastery of course material. Grades K - 12 math courses and grades 6 - 12 writing tutorials.
> Johns Hopkins University
> 3400 North Charles Street
> Baltimore, MD 21218
> (410) 516-0277
> www.jhu.edu/gifted/cde

4) See Chapter Twelve.

5) Sykes, Charles J. and William G. Durden (199_). *Questions for Your Child's School.* You've got to send for this free booklet! Thoughtful and provoking questions. The authors unabashedly advocate a rigorous, demanding education that emphasizes traditional academic subject areas. Homeschoolers: are we providing appropriately? Order an extra copy for a friend with children in public school. It's an excellent tool. Write to:
> Office of Public Information
> Center for Talented Youth
> Johns Hopkins University
> 2701 N. Charles Street
> Baltimore, MD 21218

*"Why should children of unusual abilities experience trouble with ordinary school curricula? Precisely because the curricula **are** ordinary. Education is a mass enterprise geared by economic necessity as well as politics to the abilities of the majority."*

- Dr. Harold C. Lyon, Jr.
Director of Education for the Gifted and Talented
U.S. Office of Education, January 1974

Chapter Three
Homeschooling 101

While simply rearing a gifted child may seem challenging enough, the idea of homeschooling one may seem overwhelming. Let's look at some aspects of homeschooling and you'll see that with some prayer and with some thought, you **can** do this. We'll go over some of the many options in homeschooling, some disadvantages of homeschooling, and then the decision itself.

Homeschooling is actively taking responsibility for the education of your child Perhaps you've already been doing some homeschooling without realizing it. The course that homeschooling takes depends upon your goals for your child, his or her interests and learning style, your teaching style and interests, your family schedule, and other more individual needs.

Homeschooling Options

Homeschooling schedules
Homeschooling:
Most homeschoolers are full-time at home and primarily study, work, and play there, although many attend various activities away from home like sports, music, field trips, science class, nature hikes, etc.

Afterschooling:
Some people afterschool by teaching their children after school or on Saturdays in order to keep them on track or challenged.

Part-time homeschooling: Some people take their children out of school part-time in order to be able to meet all of their needs.

Teachers: who are they?
Most elementary homeschoolers are taught by a parent. Some are taught by grandparents, and others attend co-ops where they learn things like Latin or physical education. High schoolers might also be taught by others in the community, through individual study, or in one of a number of other ways, and sometimes by combinations of all of these options.

How much planning do you personally want to do?
How much can you rely upon preplanned curricula?
Options include:
Correspondence schools: "They" do the planning, grading, pacing, and

recording. Many are available with various combinations of options and degrees of independence. Most of these do not allow deviation from the age/grade progression of their curricula. See Appendix A.

Canned curricula: The planning is done. You buy text, tests, plans, and implement them on your own. You make placing decisions and do record keeping. These are generally planned for normal children, though.

Textbooks: You buy books and whatever materials you want and use them as you wish. You keep records. You may teach or allow the student to work his or her own way through the texts.

Unit studies: You can do unit studies on your own or register with academies which keep records for you and help with planning and pacing. Within a unit study program you have many options to choose from, and most use many outside materials and library trips. If you choose to do unit studies independently, anticipate extra time for planning.

Umbrella schools: They are like correspondence schools except that most do not do the grading. Many use many different sources for materials. Like correspondence schools, umbrella schools are usually using age/grade locked curriculum and offer few choices in levels. Fifth grade is usually fifth grade in all subjects with no alternatives. A few offer independent pacing, though. A few allow unit studies. There is one designed for gifted children with individualized programming. (1)

Eclectic Method: This means you pick and choose your own texts or units or combinations to use. You decide upon pacing, level, and grade level progression. You may use any of an infinite number of combinations of methods. For instance, you may decide to use traditional math, independent art and music, unit studies for social studies, an on-line course for programming, and projects with Dad for science. This is the choice of many experienced homeschoolers.

There are many options for successful homeschooling. You can even hop back and forth between methods as you discover what works best for your child (and your schedule). Many new homeschoolers start with a canned curriculum and go on to a more eclectic style later on as they gain confidence. The important thing to remember is that you get to make the choices and that it is OK. Your own family situation is distinctive, and with a gifted child, even more so. As parents, you may be the only two people who truly have a handle on what you need to cover and how you need to do it.

After you realize that you have options, it's time to think about styles of homeschooling and your gifted child. There are philosophies of homeschooling which you can study and discuss, but it boils downs to this: your child will need some independence in schooling just as much as he or she will need the benefit of your own wisdom. Each family will use a different combination of parent-led and student-led activities. You can be confident that your own style will be best for your own family.

What will you teach? Reading, math, social studies, spelling, science, language arts, foreign languages, music and art, physical education, and spiritual training, in addition to anything else you want to cover. (No, you don't have to do all of these at once!) But what do you do for your gifted child that is different than what you would do for any child? In one sense, you will be doing exactly the same as for any child - you will be individualizing your child's education, only for a gifted child the specifics are a bit different.

Disadvantages of Homeschooling

Yes, there are disadvantages to homeschooling. They are easy to remedy, but you should be aware of them. The time element and physical fitness are problems homeschoolers may have. Non-problems (really more myths of homeschooling than problems) are socialization, laboratory science, and college entrance.

The first is the lack of a definite time schedule. In the real world, deadlines are very important. At home, though, it's easy to put off finishing a paper or a project. There are so many important things which get in the way, and it can start like this:

> *Oh, I know the paper is due on Friday, but Thursday night is Scouts, Thursday morning is the dentist appointment, and Wednesday we have church. So you can turn it in on Monday....OK, You can have until Tuesday because we had to fix the washer today...All right, Wednesday..... - Anon. Mom!*

Use a few definite deadlines for Junior which, if missed, carry a consequence. Procrastinating is a hard habit to break, especially for those of us Moms who have trouble with it anyway!

The second disadvantage is the necessity for a rigorous physical education program. Many homeschoolers rely on a soccer team as the only workout of the year. Children need a well-rounded program. There are several available in the homeschool market. (More in Chapter Five.)

Non-problems:

<u>Legality:</u> Is it legal? This used to be a commonly asked question. Now, most know it's not a problem. Yes, it is legal to homeschool in the United States. Each state has its own rules, laws, or policies. (2)

<u>Socialization:</u> This is the greatest non-problem for homeschoolers. The average homeschooled child is far better socialized than is a regular schooled child and research is beginning to reflect this. (3) Check out Brian Ray's latest publication for more data if you are curious, but children who have been homeschooled for several years appear more confident, more curious, more energetic, and relate more easily to any age group than do regularly schooled children. (4)

<u>Science laboratory:</u> This is another non-problem since there are now lab manuals especially written for homeschoolers. There are also many suppliers of science equipment for homeschooling. (5)

<u>College entrance:</u> Homeschoolers are getting into colleges and universities all across the USA and many are getting top scholarships to boot.

<u>Armed Forces:</u> Homeschoolers are now welcome in the military. Contact HSLDA for more information. (2)

The Decision

One reason people hesitate to homeschool their gifted child is because they're somewhat intimidated by the child's intelligence. When Junior is in the upper stratosphere of intelligence the parents may be afraid they won't know how to teach him, and worry that their child will lose respect for them. This is an understandable concern. But, consider this: regardless of intellect, we're to be in authority over our children. We're to teach them to honor and obey us. If we abdicate that responsibility out of fear, what are we teaching them? Also, our age gives us certain wisdom and maturity that no six or 16-year-old can have.

> *Although my children may soar above me mathematically, I have skills they haven't begun to acquire yet! I can appreciate their abilities without feeling insecure, because I realize it's a gift. It doesn't make them better people, it just makes them quicker at math problems, which I try to use to my advantage! (Quick guys - which brand of soap is a better buy?) - Maggie*

The decision to homeschool your child isn't an easy one. In fact, it takes great courage, but the rewards are incalculable. Consider your own child and his or her characteristics when thinking about your choices. Many of us have had terrible problems trying to adapt to the regular school environment and so were basically forced into the homeschooling arena, but in the end we have learned the remarkable truth: that homeschooling is a wonderful option with the potential to meet all the needs of our gifted children. Homeschooling isn't just one solution or one possibility; it's a multitude of options. Acceleration, enrichment, family values training, freedom from time pressure, time for dreaming, time for growing up at his own rate, time for personal projects, and freedom from peer pressure are all within reach at home. (6)

> *One thing no one told me about before we took our four highly gifted children out of school was that they would re-bond as a family and revert to the personal characteristics they each showed before entering school. The strong curiosity, the patience with siblings, and happy-go-lucky attitudes of the young all came back. If I had known what would transpire none of them would ever have been in any other school. Nobody told me, so I'm telling you: expect changes for the good when you take them out of school.*
> *- Kathleen*

Consider the following before deciding whether to homeschool:
- Do I want the best education possible, uniquely fitted to my child?
- Am I willing to take time to search out appropriate curriculum and resources?
- Am I willing to take time to train my child to become a lifelong, independent learner?
- Do I have support? (Spouse, family, friends, church, or others?) If not, am I willing to go it alone while continuing to seek support?
- Am I willing to make financial sacrifices in order to provide my child with what is needed?
- Am I committed to my child's education?
- Do I show respect for myself in front of my child? And -
- Does my child respect me? (These questions are related.)
- Am I willing to discard age-level curriculum planning and advancement?
- Will I let my child mature emotionally as well as academically at his own rate?
- Am I willing to be innovative?
- Am I willing to try and become consistent in all of the above?

Resources & Notes

1) The Westbridge Academy
   1610 West Highland Avenue #228
   Chicago, IL 60660
   (773) 743-3312
   westbrga@aol.com
   www.flash.net/~wx3o/westbridge/

This umbrella school is especially designed for gifted and highly motivated homeschoolers. Classical and individually-planned education.
Unit study type approaches acceptable.

2) If you're not sure of the legal requirements for home education in your state or who you might contact in your area to join a support group, get in touch with HSLDA. They'll provide you with all the necessary information. This is a tremendous organization and worthy of support.
   Home School Legal Defense Association
   PO Box 3000
   Purcellville, VA 20134
   (540) 338-5600
   www.hslda.org

3) See Chapter Five for more on socialization and homeschooling.

4) Ray, Dr. Brian (1993). *Strengths of Their Own: Homeschoolers across America: Academic Achievement, Family Characteristics, and Longitudinal Traits*. Socialization research done on homeschoolers. This booklet is a great source of concrete data on homeschoolers overall. Test averages, socioeconomic information, parental education, and more.
   National Home Education Research Institute (NHERI)
   P.O. Box 13939
   Salem, OR 97309

5) See Appendix B for companies that specialize in science materials and lab manuals and other curriculum needs.

6) For articles on homeschooling gifted, contact Kathi Kearney, founder of the Hollingworth Center for Highly Gifted Children:
   Department of Curriculum & Instruction
   N-103 Lagomarcino Hall,
   Iowa State University
   Ames, IA 50011
   kkearny@istate.edu

Chapter Four
Characteristics of Gifted Children, Learning Styles, and Homeschooling

You found a list of characteristics of gifted children in Chapter One. Some of them probably describe your student. Return to that list and note those characteristics which describe something about your child. Then leave space for notes about your child's learning characteristics to help you in the planning process. As we go over some of the more interesting characteristics, please jot down specific ideas which you find useful for schooling.

Is your child a question-asker?
We hope so. This is so important for education that we would wonder if non-question-askers even graduate from college! Although asking questions seems to come naturally to a gifted preschooler (probably most preschoolers), it's often lost in the process of going to school. Encourage this characteristic. Listen to your child and try to answer his or her questions. Resist rolling your eyes and complaining about those unending questions. Give positive reinforcement for asking them. (We know this isn't always possible, but do try.) Ask questions in response. Ask some "I wonder why?" questions and let him or her try to hypothesize answers. Don't answer all of your child's questions. Respond occasionally with a simple, "Hmm, good question."

Is your child a perfectionist?
A perfectionist feels most comfortable when things are done according to what seems right to him or her . If the shoes aren't in the right spot, then she'll move them. If the paper isn't written to the level of neatness which a teacher seemingly expects, she's in tears. If the project seems overwhelmingly hard, then he may wait until the last minute to begin (or even later). Sometimes a baby will refuse to crawl because he can't walk, or delay trying something new for fear of failure. You can see that the level of perfectionism in a child is very important to that child's schooling. Somehow we must communicate to the child, at the **feelings** level, that it's all right to fail. The world will not end and your child will not be a failure as a person if he makes mistakes.

A young person who has a difficult time with self-expectation should be encouraged to neither quit a project nor to spend unreasonable amounts of time making a project "just right." This is a fine line to walk, but you can help your student by:

❑ Allowing him reasonable time to complete a project.

❑ Encouraging her to try something which cannot be done "perfectly."

❑ Showing by example that you can laugh when something isn't "right."

❑ Expecting him or her to apologize when in the wrong, and doing the same yourself.

❑ Forgiving your child when he's apologized for something. (This reflects our Father's forgiveness, too.)

❑ Teaching her it's OK (even fun!) to play in the mud.

❑ Helping to establish time limits for the completion of projects or assignments.

❑ Understanding that not every problem has to be done correctly, (or redone until correct).

❑ Helping him stay on task even when it's a long or complicated one.

❑ Helping your child have "closure" on a project.

Some perfectionists are "organizationally impaired." These perfectionists never achieve the great results they imagine because of an inability to plan. This is a difficult problem for a perfectionist, and he will sometimes even give up trying.

One of the hardest things for anyone to say is "I'm sorry." In order to say these words, one must admit he has failed in some way, and for the gifted perfectionist, that's hard. The gifted perfectionist will need to learn to forgive himself, forgive others, and to accept forgiveness.

Perfectionism can be a trial for a gifted adult, but it can also drive that adult to greater heights of accomplishment. Thankfully, Thomas Edison did not quit his experiments on lighting sources.

Perfectionism is a term which usually carries negative connotations, but it can also lead to great achievement.

Does your child react with intense emotions to reasonably normal situations or overreact to abnormal ones?
Why is it that a 4-year-old can feel badly because her mother has been insulted? How can a youngster of that age have "hurt feelings" for someone else? It certainly happens. This characteristic is sometimes called "over-excitability," and it's normal.

Gifted children can show emotional responses that seem out of proportion to their cause. What do you tell a sad 3-year-old child whose dog just died when he asks whether Skippy is going to heaven or not? What does this have to do with learning? A child who needs to have answers to these kinds of questions is one who also will need to understand what causes war, the reason people die in famines, or why Booth shot Lincoln. A slightly older child may desperately struggle with the issue of fairness, or the existence of God.

Expect your gifted child to need answers to questions like these, even if you don't have them. They will need to talk about some of these things. Your younger gifted child may need a reassuring hug or two to let him know he's safe with his family in spite of what he hears on the evening news. Teach him critical thinking and logic early. Pray with him. Choose texts which list causes of events and their results. Help him understand the big picture of world history. You will demonstrate your solid faith in God and, in addition, teach him to manage his emotions.

In an adult, this emotional supersensitivity can be expressed in many ways, but it all points to a wonderful ability to understand people and their doings. Adults with this well-controlled characteristic can understand motives, help people with emotional problems, or track criminals. Other adults with this gift can paint with words, make an instrument sing, or lead others in government.

Intense emotions can be a characteristic at once hard to live with, but with many rewards.

Does your child have high energy levels?
Do you feel like you run at full tilt just to keep up with him? Does he sleep like a log and once awake, hit the ground running? If you have other children, you may find yourself using a tether in the grocery store. This child must be watched from an early age (as soon as they can crawl), and can set a record for miles covered on hands and knees.

An older child may be misdiagnosed as ADD, ADHD, or simply hyperactive, especially by a frustrated teacher. Many gifted children are tested for hyperactivity precisely because of this characteristic. In fact, it's an extremely common trait in gifted children, especially the highly gifted. You can usually tell that the problem is not ADD (or whatever the current term is), by asking yourself: "Is it only when he's interested in the topic, or bored, or is it all the time?" "Is the activity directed or totally unfocused?" Many gifted children are very intense about dinosaurs and able to spend long, peaceful hours on their Legos™ while totally non-interested in their schoolwork because of boredom. The teacher, seeing a non-compliant child, thinks "hyperactive." High energy levels are great for the adult focused on a major project. Remember that the characteristics of the child will eventually be reflected in the adult, so take heart. There is value in this trait.

Does your child need little sleep?
Even when you need more? This is especially hard on Mom when the little gifted one is a baby, perhaps undiagnosed as gifted as yet, but gifted nonetheless. A 5-month-old may be up from a nap after only thirty minutes down. Some little ones take naps only when exhausted, their interests keeping them up long past when their bodies say it is time to sleep. Some mothers even complain of babies who never nap during the day. A 6-year-old may be up early and into trouble, taking apart Grandma's camera or Dad's model.

How does energy level affect schooling? Be prepared to move around: study plants by taking a hike outside instead of looking at a book, or take frequent breaks to incorporate some physical activity. Allow him time to study peacefully when the need arises, or when curiosity takes over. If you need a break from the intensity level, require your little one to lay down with a book; to nap, if possible. Remember - take your vitamins!

The long term benefit of those high energy levels is, of course, the ability to follow through on a research project or a book. It takes a long time to complete some things and energy level is very important.

Does she seem to have heightened senses?
Can she hear everything you say (especially when you don't want to be overheard)? One mother recently told me she had to homeschool her child because his hearing had been measured at the zero decibel level; that is, he heard everything. Needless to say, this was a problem for him at school. Some children can discern a flicker in the TV or in the computer monitor. Some can only use the best monitors because of this problem. Other children must have fluorescent lights instead of incandescent because of the "yellow" light incandescent lights give off. This is the same trait that forces your child to complain until you cut the tag from his shirt. What about the child who must have that little seam in her socks on the top of her foot, or on the bottom, or wherever?

> *Esther refused to wear shoes until we figured out a way to get them on her. Daniel refused to tie his shoes, or rather, he refused to re-tie them, so instead, he just left them tied all the time. We finally got smart and bought velcro fastening shoes. What was so hard to understand was that these were normally obedient children. What we did not know was that this type of behavior was not a discipline problem but rather a gifted problem. - Kathleen*

Finally, a name for this characteristic: supersensitivity!

For school, this trait can be a problem until you understand the cause. A child may need a book with color for visual cues. A book with too much on any page may be a trial. Think about the child you're buying for when you choose texts, notebooks, curtains, even lighting. It may make all the difference to your schooling. You can build a good learning environment for your gifted child; it just takes thought, and yes, persistence.

Great sensitivity can help an artist choose just the right shade of color, or a photographer understand just the right lighting. It may merely mean that your gifted adult can "see" with greater depth and enjoy with greater awareness God's gifts.

Is he persistent?
Maybe stubborn is a better term? One of the most tension-producing characteristics of a bright child is his ability to stay on a subject, whether it's "Can I have dessert if I eat this additional pea?" or the random "Why? Why?", etc. Mom, remember, two can play that game. A child who likes to make the decisions can make a good one when choices are provided by his on-top-of-the-situation parent. There's no rule that says we can't manipulate, too! Positive reinforcement is a great way to get your child to finish a task. (Some may call stickers, stamps, and Oreos™ bribery, while others call it positive reinforcement.) An important rule of thumb is: don't let your child make all the decisions. He may be gifted, but you're the parent! Besides, according to *What We Have Learned About Gifted Children,* (1) statistically speaking, parents of gifted children are probably gifted, too. (2)

> *Persistence is rarely welcome in young children. We had an unwritten assumption in our house that flying was something women did as well as men. Our four-year-old Joseph once argued for twenty-four hours that only "daddies" could be pilots. His evidence? Only that his mom, though a pilot herself, didn't wear an Air Force flight suit. - Kathleen*

These characteristics of gifted children usually aren't listed and may not sound exactly complementary, but which are nonetheless true characteristics, and commonly observed in gifted children. These traits are important in planning for school, because of the many ways they impact schooling. To the level that you direct or manage these characteristics, you will succeed in rearing a gifted child who will become a balanced, gifted adult.

Resources and Notes

1) Silverman, Linda in a paper <u>What We Have Learned About Gifted Children</u>, published in 1997 and delivered in a speech at the NAGC (National Association for Gifted Children) Conference in November, 1997, in Little Rock, Arkansas.

2) Silverman, Linda in the above noted paper states:
"Where one child in the family is found to be gifted, the chances are great that all members of the family are gifted. Brothers and sisters are usually within five to ten points in ability. We studied 48 sets of siblings and found that over one-third were within five points of each other, over three-fifths were within ten points, and almost three-quarters were within thirteen points..... Parents' IQ scores, when known, are usually within ten points of their children's; grandparents' IQ scores are often within ten points of their grandchildren's."

Question:
Do you think school is easier for you than most people?

Answers:
Probably not, because I have my distractions, too.
- Scott Von Duyke, age 9

No, I've got my weaknesses - just like anybody else.
- Andrew Johnson, age 15

Chapter Five
Schooling the Whole Child -
More Than a Brain

It's all too easy to get caught up in the academic arena with bright kids. Naturally, we want them to do their best work, and we want to provide a high quality of education. But, we don't want lopsided children either; all brain and no personality! Some other aspects to their development that need to be considered are:

- Spiritual Life
- Emotional and Behavioral Development
- Physical Fitness
- Service to Others
- Hobbies
- Social Life
- Fine Arts, Esthetics
- Requirements for Adulthood

Spiritual Life

Are you discipling your gifted child? They will see very quickly if your faith is real; if you're "walking the walk or just talking the talk." Modeling is important for all our children, but again, gifted youngsters are incredibly perceptive. We ought to be the role models they need.

PRACTICAL APPLICATIONS

✞ Include Bible studies as part of your daily schooling. (1)

✞ Read a family devotional book together at dinner or bedtime. Perhaps Dad could assume this responsibility, if he's not already doing so.

✞ Attend a house of worship on a regular basis.

✞ Do Bible memory work and play "trivia" or memory games. (2)

✞ If you see prideful attitudes related to giftedness, address this character issue firmly and consistently. Our world needs bright leaders who are immersed in Scripture, not in self.

✞ Practice love and forgiveness with them and with others.

Emotional and Behavioral Development

Emotional development is so individual and so subjective that none of us feel enough expertise to cover it. But, there are a few comments we would like to make. Gifted children are, like any children, sensitive to their environment, both family and community. Some gifted children are extremely sensitive to the world around them. God has given us these children and put them into our care so that we can protect them while allowing them to mature at their own rates. The development of gifted children is influenced by their emotional development, both rate differences and sensitivities.

RATE DIFFERENCES, OR ASYNCHRONY:
The rate at which gifted children develop emotionally is, like all children, always changing. This means that they grow emotionally in spurts much as they do physically. In addition to being out of synch with age peers, your gifted child may be out of synch with herself or himself. A family may have a 5-year-old who can understand and cry about death and war, yet has the insecurities of a normal 5-year-old who sucks his thumb and has a blankey. This kind of developmental confusion is a problem which is easier to solve at home in a loving, nurturing environment where parents can explain things and pray with their child. (3)

SENSITIVITY:
In the profoundly gifted ranges, and even in the more normally gifted child, sensitivity to the environment can appear abnormal, while in actuality it's very normal and the child merely needs a more solid, nurturing environment. The regular school setting can be emotionally stressing to a very sensitive child. Many parents report that their children complain of illness just to avoid going to school. The gifted child may beg parents to homeschool him. Others report ulcers and other stress-related illnesses. Complaining to get out of school is a type of avoidance behavior which has been used for centuries. Another type of behavior is a withdrawal; for example, a student who wore a drover's coat at all times during school hours. This behavior, too, ended when the student was surrounded by a more welcoming environment. Both avoidance and withdrawal behaviors are signs that something is wrong with the environment that the child is trying to escape. It's important not to let these signs go without response. If you have questions about social and emotional support for the gifted child, consider calling Supporting The Emotional Needs of the Gifted (SENG). (4)

Note: Most children leaving regular school will need a "de-tox" period to become familiar with the homeschooling freedoms and responsibilities.

For a few, this can be traumatic and may be accompanied by emotional upheavals. This will usually last about three months, if it occurs at all. Have patience; time and understanding will do wonders.

> *One of mine wasn't enthusiastic about homeschooling since she had gotten into the social life of junior high. She would announce (loudly) that her real teachers didn't do algebra that way and leave the room. After a little time out and understanding, she would wander back into our work room and get back to her math. Over time, this behavior ended and she became a part of the family again.*
> *- Kathleen*

Physical Fitness

"Jogging is very beneficial. It's good for your legs and your feet. It's also very good for the ground. It makes it feel needed."

- Charles M. Schultz

★ Modeling is crucial! Get in shape yourself as you work with them.

★ Let physical fitness become a regular part of your curriculum. Develop a plan for fitness. Pick practical options your children will enjoy. So many choices await you...everything from video aerobic exercise, to classes at the YMCA, to rope jumping and bike riding.

★ Children need regular exercise that includes an aerobic activity to help them get and stay fit. Post a fitness chart and fill out exercise, eating, and health habits daily.

★ Gifted kids are sometimes stereotyped as frail bookworms. Make a point of teaching your children rules to common, neighborhood games like kickball, steal-the-bacon, foursquare, hopscotch, and touch football.

★ If possible, give them opportunities to experience at least one team sport. For instance, soccer is popular and available almost everywhere.

★ Tennis classes, bowling leagues, and roller skating are other good possibilities. Knowledge of common forms of recreation allow the homeschooled gifted child to more easily blend when in group situations.

★ Indoor exercise equipment may provide the easiest way for consistent exercise, but provide them with other opportunities occasionally, too.

★ Gymnastics centers, roller rinks, bowling alleys, YMCA's, and health clubs are potential outlets for homeschool classes. They may have slow times during the day, which they'd love to fill. Provide them with the kids and they should provide you with quality classes at discount prices.

✫ Martial arts are a popular form of exercise. We know one homeschool group that gets discounted day rates, and the homeschool classes contain no form of meditations, mantras, or other questionable activities, just good, clean exercise. Added bonus: many parents can take classes with their kids.

Three parts of a good physical fitness plan are:
→ Aerobics for cardio-respiratory health
→ Stretching for flexibility
→ Exercises or weight training for strength building

Service to Others

"To whom much is given, much is required." Gifted kids need to know that they have their particular abilities for a reason and that they need to be open to God's calling in their lives. It's exciting to imagine the different ways these talented young people may choose to serve!

Brainstorm for service projects that can be done individually and/or as a family. Choose a few and make arrangements to carry them out. Depending on the age of the child, they may be able to make most or even all of the arrangements on their own. Organizing and following through with any project is a valuable skill.

A FEW IDEAS TO GET YOU ROLLING:

✦ Collect items for low-income day cares, homeless shelters, or poor/ elderly folks.

✦ Raise money for a specific need: Project Angel Tree (5), Make A Wish Foundation (6), soup kitchens.

✦ Volunteer: at the hospital, library, nursing home, Society for the Prevention of Cruelty to Animals, church nursery.

✦ Be a good neighbor: adopt a single mom or older and/or handicapped person. Take care of their mail, or yard work, dusting, or shopping. Kids can write letters for older folk, or be a mother's helper for that struggling, single mom. All this implies volunteering, of course - no money is involved.

✦ What can be done at home? Write encouraging notes on a regular basis to folks who could really use them - the bereaved, lonely, elderly, new to town, housebound, etc. Become a "Telephone Pal" to a shut-in to provide

"Sports do not build character, they reveal it."

-Heywood Brown

them with outside communication, and check in daily or weekly to see how they're doing. A child can save funny stories, interesting news, and family anecdotes to share with their "pal" each week.

✈ For relatively little money you can adopt a child through one of the many relief organizations. (7) What a wonderful way to show and model love and mercy!

✈ Our kids have done many different types of volunteer work. They're learning that the reward lies in the sense of satisfaction that comes with doing something from the heart, the selfless act. But they've also had unexpected rewards: paying jobs and other happy experiences. Regardless of the rewards, serving others is an important lesson that can be passed down to our children.

Hobbies

Bright kids love hobbies. Sometimes it's one, all-consuming passion; baseball cards, horses, dinosaurs, rocks, space, dolls. Sometimes they enjoy a variety of hobbies. Hobbies bring a needed balance to the academic life, and are wonderful avenues to explore interests in a nonthreatening, stress-free way. Encourage them to explore a variety of activities as the opportunity arises, but hobbies aren't the place to push, push, push. Consider some past-times particularly appropriate for stretching the horizons of bright minds, like:

Chess	Baseball card collecting
Aquariums	Stamp & postcard collecting
Foreign languages for fun	Other collections
Animal husbandry	Meteorology
Sign language	Astronomy
Bridge	Oceanography
Crossword puzzles	Art
Model building	Writing
Genealogy	Music
Cooking/baking	
Electronics	

Social Life

"But what about socialization?" That question always pops up! There's a stereotype that homeschooled kids are "socially maladjusted." There's another stereotype that gifted kids are "weird." Put them together and you may get some pretty strange reactions to homeschooling Georgie the Genius! Besides, just because Georgie is a genius, it doesn't mean he's gifted in the area of social skills.

Naturally, these stereotypes are for the most part unfounded, but we have seen times when it is all too true. We've spoken with a few homeschooled teens now in college who've said it can be painfully embarrassing how easily they can pick out other homeschooled teens. - Janice

As a contrary voice, Daniel and Sarah both have told me that they can spot homeschooled kids too, but not because of the lack of social awareness. It's because the homeschooled children are more outgoing, confident, and can come up with many ideas for the group to do. The regularly schooled teens (or homeschoolers who have recently come out of regular schools) tend to be disinterested and unable to suggest activities. - Kathleen

We need to make a positive impact on this world, not a negative one. Here are some practical suggestions for helping Georgie fit in:

❀Practice social situations ahead of time. Can Georgie perform a proper introduction? Is he comfortable with both adults and peers? Does he know how to behave in restaurants or out in public?

❀ Does your older child know how to look someone in the eyes when speaking to them?

❀ Do they shake hands at appropriate times, speak clearly, and practice social conventions like opening doors for ladies, elderly people, etc.?

❀ Do they know how to speak politely without going overboard and sounding like Little Miss Manners?

❀ Is your child competent on the phone? Simple phone etiquette:
   ◇　Answer politely and clearly.
   ◇ When retrieving someone for a phone call, don't shout into the receiver or place the receiver down hard on a surface.

"I pay the School Master, but 'tis the boys that educate my son."

-Ralph Waldo Emerson

◇ If the party called cannot come to the phone, simply say so. (Not, "Mommy's going potty right now.")

◇ Offer to take a message.

◇ Record phone messages accurately, repeating back names and phone numbers.

● It may be wise to check out a few etiquette books and review them occasionally. Good manners will help a person through many difficult situations in the course of their lifetime. Teach them.

● Observe your children in group situations. Are they comfortable? If not, why not? Observe the problems and discuss them later. Role playing acceptable behavior may be helpful for youngsters who really have trouble with fitting into a group. (We don't mean a "gang," but simple social settings like story hour, Sunday school, or scouts.)

● If, after much effort, your child truly seems a misfit, look for a good counseling service in your area. Some children simply need more intense training in interpersonal relationships. These skills will be a lifelong blessing to them. Check with trusted friends or your church for recommendations.

All children go through stages, and some can go through periods of almost painful shyness. One of the advantages of homeschooling is that we can allow children to mature at their own pace, not according to some group's average maturation process. Most shyness will be outgrown, but it never hurts to talk to your child about her uneasiness. If you have any serious concerns, go to the experts: a mom who has "been there", or a counselor. Focus on the Family can provide good advice and give you names of Christian counselors in your area. (8)

Homeschooled students are doing just fine socially, according to a recent study done by homeschool researcher Vicki Tillman. (9)

> "Study on homeschoolers' socialization and self-esteem was initiated less than a decade ago. The benchmark study was by Taylor (1986). Using self-concept as measured on the Piers-Harris Self-Concept Scale, he found that the self-concept of homeschooled children was significantly higher than that of the norms on the global scale. The median for the home schooled sample was the 91st percentile." (10)

All studies we've seen on the socialization of homeschoolers gives the same positive news: homeschoolers are definitely "socially acceptable"!

Fine Arts

It's good to be able to appreciate art and artists, both musical and visual. In order to do that, children need to be able to recognize art, point out the qualities of that art, and try their hands at producing some of it. If you're artistically challenged, this is hard to do. Actually, it isn't hard to do; it's just hard to know **what** to do. Check out local museums for art classes and tours. Study major artists and musicians from the past and become familiar with their work. Provide your child with opportunities to draw, play an instrument, and learn to read music This is believed to enhance one's ability to think. Other ideas abound:

•❖Invest in quality drawing materials from the local art store: pencils, colored pencils, charcoal, a variety of paper, sketch pads, etc.

•❖Obtain a list of drawing projects from the local art teacher or from a book about drawing. Draw leaves, your hand, your foot, someone else, your dog, a stool, a flower, a landscape, your house, a lamp, an abstract, a pattern of lines or of shapes, a drawing of a face in outline, etc.

•❖ Study the elements of art in order to be able to evaluate art. (11)

•❖ Go to the museum for classes.

•❖ Take a tour and make notes.

•❖ Visit a museum and copy one piece of art. Just sit down and draw it.

•❖ Learn to dance.

•❖Attend performances of the local orchestra.

•❖ Learn to play an instrument (even a recorder).

•❖ Frequent lectures by performers, docents, or other people on music, art, theater, etc.

•❖Attend plays, especially Shakespearean. Perform in plays.

•❖ Learn the art of photography

•❖ Learn to decorate.

Requirements for Adulthood

Skills adults need are excellent topics to cover at home:

banking procedures	child care
loans	nutrition and cooking
investing	clothing care
budgeting	first aid
taxes	cardio-pulmonary resuscitation (CPR)
auto maintenance	lifesaving and water safety
minor or major auto repair	organizational skills
sewing (or tailoring)	insurance savvy
cleaning	

Add your own ideas to this list and develop your own family list of requirements for adulthood. Include aspects of life your child will need to function well as an adult. Topics most gifted children would never study in regular school, homeschoolers can cover at home.

> *Our two oldest children rebuilt an MG Midget with Dad. All helped recover our Taylorcraft airplane. They all had bank accounts (and bounced the requisite number of checks before learning how to prevent it). They learned the basics of sewing, cooking, auto repair, first aid, and CPR. The two youngest wrote their own books, attended small business seminars with me, and socked away earnings for college. - Kathleen*

Make your own list and use it to plan for the next year. A friend's children are required to donate a certain number of hours at a local school for retarded adults. Another family requires their children to learn about nutrition and herbal medicines.

Take the time to think through your goals. You may even find it helpful to post them in a conspicuous place to help your family stay on track.

Resources & Notes:

1) *Precepts Bible Study* by Kay Arthur. Inductive Bible studies for the middle school ages through adult. Widely available at Christian bookstores.

2) Memlok Bible Memory System™. Topical Bible memorization based on flash cards with pictures symbolizing the first words of each verse.

Well-Versed Kids. Simple, easy to use. Three levels of difficulty for children.

3) Dobson, Dr. James, Focus on the Family Publications
(800) AFamily

4) SENG - Supporting the Emotional Needs of the Gifted
College of Continuing Studies
Kent State University
PO Box 5190
Kent, OH 44242-0001
www.kent.edu/

5) Project Angel Tree is a ministry to prisoners' families during the Christmas season, providing gifts for prisoners' children. You can participate on your own or through a local church.
Project Angel Tree
PO Box 16069
Washington, DC 20041-6069
(800) 398-HOPE
www.christianity.com/angeltree

6) Make-A-Wish Foundation
3550 N. Central Ave.
Suite 300
Phoenix, AZ 85012
(800) 722-9474
www.wish.org
MAWFA@wish.org

7) New Missions

PO Box 2727
Orlando, FL 32802
(800) 937-4248
www.newmissions.org
Haiti@NewMissions.org

We've included New Missions here because we're personally involved with them. Some of our children have been to Haiti and witnessed the fantastic work that this organization is doing and the tremendous changes that have been made in the lives of Haitians in their area. For a small monthly fee, you and your child can make a huge difference - an eternal difference - in the life of a Haitian child.

8) See note (3).

9) Home School Researcher Editor, Brian D. Ray, Ph.D.
National Home Education Research Institute (NHERI)
P.O. Box 13939
Salem, OR 97309
(503) 364-1490
www.nheri.org

10) The Home School Researcher is an excellent up-to-date resource which is dedicated to the dispersal of information relevant to the research of home education. Particularly helpful is the Vol. 11, No. 3, 1995, p.1-6, article titled "Home Schoolers, Self-Esteem, and Socialization" by Vicki D. Tillman.

11) Evaluating art can be done systematically by using the three elements: realism, impressionism, and formalism.

Question:
Do you like being homeschooled? Why?

Answer:
Yes, because:
1) there's less violence,
2) no peer pressure,
3) no exposure to diseases,
4) I can work at my own pace, and
5) no bullies.
-Matthew Matheson, age 11

My thought is that servanthood and hard work are essential qualities for gifted people. A mother, especially a homeschooling one, can wear herself out running her child to 'gifted' programs, missing the most valuable 'program' she can give him right in her own home: the gift of work and service.
-Kathy, mother of Scott, age 9

Chapter Six
Parenting the Intellectually Gifted Learner

Parenting a young gifted person can be rewarding and frustrating at the same time. The characteristics of giftedness, asynchrony, high energy levels, and intensity, tend to magnify the normal developmental stages the children go through. Let's go over a few of these differences and discuss some recommendations for parenting gifted children, especially concerning behavior patterns, siblings, disabled gifted, and discipline.

Boundaries: The importance of establishing healthy behavior patterns while children are young cannot be overstated. Children, especially academically gifted ones, need boundaries. They test and retest boundaries to ensure their security and stability. It doesn't matter that they poked at that 'section of fence' yesterday and received assurance it was intact; today's a new day! (Maybe something happened within the hour or overnight to weaken it and it must be checked again. Or maybe Mom will give in this time!)

This behavior can be exasperating and is common in gifted kids. It often seems large amounts of time are spent setting limits, checking a child's understanding of those limits and the consequences of going beyond them, and then correcting intentional disobedience and following through with prescribed consequences. This is normal and this is exhausting. But, if you're diligent in your consistency, you will be rewarded. Happy is the child who has thoroughly and persistently tested those boundaries and found them to be firm and strong; such a child will grow into a secure and obedient young adult. Our prisons are full of people who have gone through life either without any boundaries or with weak, unpatrolled boundaries, so the government must step in to provide boundaries in the form of jail cells. All children test their boundaries to some degree, but in gifted children this behavior is exaggerated.

Be careful to set the example you want your child to follow throughout childhood. For instance, if you do not wish to allow television viewing each day, then don't allow it even for the young child because you're establishing patterns that are going to be difficult to break once that child is older. Save yourself much aggravation now by carefully choosing what you will and will not allow while he's young, or you're setting yourself up for confrontation when he becomes a teenager. As Bill Gothard has correctly pointed out, **"What parents allow in moderation, children will excuse in excess."** (1)

*"Train up
a child in
the way he
should go,
and when
he is old
he will not
depart
from it."*

*-Proverbs
12:4*

Show an interest in the world around you and your child will, too. Take walks in the woods or backyard. Ask, "Wow, I wonder what kind of bird (or tree) that is?" "Can you remember the name of this pretty flower?" Or ask an older child, "What type of fungus is this? What does it indicate about the air quality in this community?" Kids love to ask questions. Gifted kids LOVE to ask and ask and ask questions. Don't answer them all! Rather, ask them questions.

I wonder why? Especially, ask them the "I wonder" questions, which teach them not only to observe, but to question. It's the ability to ask the "I wonder" questions which will enable them to succeed in college. When a student listens to an instructor, asking himself questions about the topic of the lecture, he's participating in "active listening" and will better understand concepts. A parent models this by asking herself the questions aloud. "Hmm-m-m, I wonder why they painted that sign red?" Because she has asked herself, children aren't on the spot, but they are listening and will begin to ask themselves these kind of questions. By so doing, the parent has modeled an inquisitive mind.

Keep them thinking. Talk to them. Read to them. Listen to audio tapes and be careful about the TV and the VCR. Brainwave patterns of people watching either television or movies are almost identical to the brainwave patterns of those who are asleep! That fact, combined with the reality of the pathetic condition of so much of television programming should encourage us to avoid the snare of the electronic babysitter. The siren call of the TV is especially difficult for the parent of a verbal and inquisitive gifted child to resist. Ah, the thought of it. An hour of silence! Calgon™, take me away! Nothing wrong with that occasionally, but keep in mind that you're modeling behavior to them. So plan for those times with a supply of wholesome, educational diversions. Keep their brains exercised, and they will be happier and smarter.

Siblings

Human beings compare themselves with other human beings from early childhood on. Even as adults we must fight the temptation to compare ourselves to others. Perhaps thoughts like this have crossed your mind: "I wish I could be like her. She homeschools eight children, teaches Sunday School, runs the soup kitchen, has a masters degree and is working on a doctorate, operates a home-based business, has a spotless house with meals on time every night, and she's gorgeous as well! ... And look at me."

"The aim of education is knowledge, not of facts but of value."

-William R. Inge

When we as adults, who know better, allow our thoughts to get carried away by comparisons, can we expect our children not to? The non-gifted sibling will compare himself to the gifted child. Sometimes the gifted child is delighted to assist the non-gifted one in making these comparisons. Keep in mind, however, that the non-gifted child will make comparisons even if the gifted child never does. The parents' role is not only to try to curb and deflect negative comparisons, but to discover and nurture the skill and abilities in the non-gifted child. Even two gifted siblings will make comparisons. The differences in their abilities will challenge them, and so one will ask "Why can Susan read so much better than me and when she's two years younger?"

How does this translate into practical living? Jonah is an aspiring pianist but is not a fast academic learner. He may receive music lessons or other encouragement in his talent. He is also encouraged to do his best academically, but he is not compared unfavorably to his brother Benjamin who's an academic whiz. He moves ahead in classes/grades rapidly and is encouraged in his talents without negative comparisons to Jonah. Each of us is to use what we have to the best of our ability.

Occasionally, a parent will ask one of us for advice about advancing a gifted child past or up to the level of a sibling. Each person has gifts which should not be handicapped because of the apparent needs of another. It's not fair to either child; they know when one is quicker to understand things. A parent cannot hide this, and it won't help to ignore them or to be silent about a gift. Each child deserves his own unique education. If not, eventually, one of those children will hold it against the parent. The best advice is to pray and be honest. "Yes, Susan can read better than you can. Isn't it wonderful that God gives each of us different gifts?" Give each child the best you can, and let the academically advanced child progress according to her abilities, not her sibling's.

Inside each child God has placed a "seed," and it's the parents' responsibility to provide conditions optimal for growth. It may take many years to discover what that seed will grow to be, but we must give our best effort to help it along. Poor self-image, perceived lack of ability, and shyness can all be indications that a non-gifted child has been unfavorably comparing himself with his gifted sibling and allowing the comparison to damage his self worth. A parent must continually communicate to such a child that he is worthy, that he does have abilities, that he is a wonderful person with many gifts. But make sure you mean what you say. Children have an uncanny ability to see through false flattery. Know what your child's strengths are and frequently reassure him that you believe in him, that he's important to your family, and that he's loved every bit as much as his sibling. This may be a good time to review Gardner's book on Multiple Intelligences. (2)

Look for opportunities for that child to shine. Make those opportunities. Acknowledge their accomplishments frequently to friends and relatives. Sometimes in our zeal to encourage our academically gifted kids, we forget that there are brothers and/or sisters watching and listening. They want to hear about their accomplishments and see your face light up with pride at the mention of their names. It is right and good to offer praise and encouragement to children for their accomplishments. Be sensitive in this area. Sometimes academic accomplishments are easier to see than nonacademic ones. Make certain that ALL your children know beyond any doubt that they are appreciated and treasured. (3)

Doubly Blessed: Learning Disabled and Gifted

"I know my son is very bright - but he can't sit still or concentrate for more than a few minutes."

"My child is verbally precocious, but he's nine and hasn't begun to read."

"Can my child be considered gifted even though she has a severe behavioral disorder?"

Yes! Gifted kids, just like the rest of us, come in all kinds of packages. Learning disabilities (LD), hyperactivity, Attention Deficit Disorder (ADD), and behavioral problems don't mean that a child isn't gifted.

Many of the parents we've spoken with have had concerns with hyperactivity, behavioral and learning problems. It's certainly possible to have a gifted child who is also ADD or LD, or who suffers from other behavior/learning disorders. These children are a special challenge. Of course, in order to meet their academic needs, you'll have to know how to deal appropriately with their other needs. (4)

Obviously, it is beyond the scope of this book to give advice concerning particular disorders and/or disabilities. There is professional help available and it should be sought if possible. Diagnostic tests may be available from a nearby children's hospital. Additionally Dr. Joe Sutton, a certified educational diagnostician, offers a diagnostic testing service by mail. (5) Ask trusted friends for recommendations for a counseling center that offers diagnostic testing.

Lastly, these children often require an inordinate amount of time. Giving them your best means that you must take care of yourself, too. Try to arrange for your own free time; time away to reflect, regroup, and reenergize! **Above all else, love them. Love covers many of our parental shortcomings, real or perceived!**

Discipline

This is not a book on child discipline, but there are a couple of topics which do tend to turn up repeatedly in our seminars. The first is an observation: gifted people tend to have a great ability to manipulate. Gifted children are no different. If they discover that you can be manipulated, they may try it, and they may be very successful. Parents have related stories of being taken in by very young children. The best recommendation we can give is to try not to be taken in by your brilliant youngster. It's not a good lesson for him or her to learn, and it does your image no good either! For information on the strong willed child, look to Focus on the Family. The advice of Dr. James Dobson works well for gifted children. (6)

The second topic is along the same line as the first: your children need to respect you. If you tell other people how your little genius knows so much more than you do and if your little genius hears this, he'll assume you mean it and that you really aren't very intelligent. He will then act on this assumption. This is not the image you want your child to have of you. Putting yourself down is really just a backward way to brag about the child but the actual result is far different. You don't want your child to lose respect for you. As a matter of fact, the odds are (according to research) that you're just as bright as your child, as are his siblings. (7) So, encourage your child's respect by not criticizing yourself or your spouse, and ensure his obedience. This is as important with a gifted child as with any other.

The principles of rearing children to be godly adults will work for gifted children, even though the asynchronies, intensities, and supersensitivities may interfere and discourage parents. God really does have a plan for your child and since the giftedness was His idea, the first step we should always take is to refer to the Maker for counsel.

Resources & Notes:

1) Bill Gothard as noted in Basic Youth Conflicts materials.

2) Gardner, See Chapter One, Resources and Notes.

3) Sometimes it is easy to overlook the needs of the gifted child to be accepted in our understandable desire that the non-gifted child (or "unidentified as gifted" child) feel accepted.

4) Learning disabilities information:

The International Dyslexia Association
Chester Building Suite 382
8600 LaSalle Road
Baltimore, MD 21286-2044
(410) 296-0232
(800) ABC-D123
www.interdys.org

Smart Kids with School Problems by Priscilla L. Vail (E.P.Dutton 1987) This book includes seven types of gifted identified by Gardner. Vail called gifted kids with learning disabilities "conundrum kids." They may show great promise but turn away from education because of misunderstood learning problems. Practical coping suggestions are written in an understandable, common sense way. Her chapter "Testing Demystified" was objective concerning testing for LD. If you suspect your smart kid of having learning problems, this book is worth reading.
5) Sutton, Dr. Joe

6) Dobson, Dr. James, Focus on the Family Publications

7) Silverman. See Chapter Four Notes and Resources, note (2).
The Gifted Development Center
1452 Marion Street
Denver, CO 80218
voice: (303) 837-8378
Fax: (303) 831-7465
www.gifteddevelopment.com

Chapter Seven
What To Teach, When

Many homeschoolers try to keep the same yearly schedule as a regular school. They teach math according to the scope and sequence from a curriculum publisher and do grammar every year. There are several problems with this approach, but the bottom line is that there are differences in importance between subjects. Learning to read is one of the most important skills your child can acquire; far more important than geometry, for example. Some subjects are simply vital to learning every other subject. These are the tools of the trade:

Tools of the Trade

Reading & Comprehension	Arithmetic Skills	Spelling	Handwriting
Maps & Charting Skills	How to Listen	How to Ask Questions	How to Pray

Teach the tools of the trade first, reinforce them often, and test them for mastery. In the first part of your planning sequence, evaluate your student in these areas. There are diagnostics available for this. You may be surprised at the 'holes' regular school has left in your child's education. Occasionally, specific learning disabilities will appear in these areas. These "holes" are the skills to re-mediate if missing or incomplete.

If you have a young child, these topics may be all you cover. If you have limited time for schooling, concentrate on getting these done and filling in with the other topics. Get these done early and spend the rest of the time on the really fun things. Many gifted children learn the tools of the trade easily, often with little or no instruction.

You've tested your child and have the results. Next, decide on grade levels according to the testing. Susan, a second grader, may be studying:

Spelling: second grade level.
Reading: books from a classic book list.
Math: using EPGY at the fourth grade level.
Handwriting: practice book from second grade level.
Maps & Charts: using material from Bright Ideas Press. (1)
History: unit studies, historical biographies, museums, reenactments, etc.
Science: *Hands-on Science* (2) or *The Scientist's Apprentice* (3)
Bible: family devotionals with Bible stories.

This plan meets the Tools of the Trade list, gives Susan some independent work (history and science, maps, handwriting, and any other project she can come up with), and leaves time for plenty of growing, reading, and playing. It also meets her needs in challenging level and pacing (math and reading), depth of content (historical and scientific studies), and complexity (through your discussions with her, especially in Bible, reading, history, and science). Susan could drop spelling and the map study, substituting an independent project of her choice.

Another example: Joshua, a 12-year-old with an energetic mom, will be doing a unit study which includes art history, science, history, literature and more, but which requires more of her time. He will do math by using a normal text and manipulatives, spelling by choosing misspelled words from his compositions and journal, and science by a nature journal to supplement his unit work. This is a lot of fun - for both of them. It's also a lot of work, some of which could be eliminated or substituted for more independent work. While his mom's enjoying the challenge and excitement of this schedule now, later she may want to re-evaluate her school schedule if it doesn't seem to be working well, if she needs time for another project, or if she's not comfortable with it for any reason.

Our children are each different. The child who enjoys journaling is one who writes easily, but some of our gifted children may not be like this; in fact, they may not like that kind of activity all. Also, not every child learns best with manipulatives, and just because the guy at the book fair says it's the best way, that may not be true for your child.

Plan with the child in mind, not the curriculum.

Here are more tools you'll be tempted to have your six-year-old using, but which aren't as necessary at that age as the Tools of the Trade. Add these now or a little later, depending on your own plan. Notice that we don't have grades on these lists, taking into account the individuality of each family of homeschoolers.

More Tools

O Grammar.
O An idea of the sequence of time and historical events.
O Observational science (or descriptive science) and science skills. (4)
O Scripture memory and Bible stories.
O Advanced Arithmetic skills.
O A musical instrument or voice.
O Mathematical reasoning. (5)
O Geography skills. (6)

Still later, perhaps at nine or ten, you might add:

O Composition.
O Advanced memory work (poems, Bible, states and capitals, important source documents, etc.).
O Typing, cursive, library research skills.
O Reading aloud.
O Working puzzles (hard ones).
O Great books, including classics.
O Latin.
O Gymnastics.

Your preadolescent may be able to start high school level material, plus:

O Serious work on the details of history and science.
O Vocabulary work.
O Latin: Real, classical Latin, not just the "roots." (When we studied Latin, we didn't worry about grammar or vocabulary in English.)
O Finish arithmetic and do puzzles, problem solving, geometry, and business math (pre-algebra topics).
O Making speeches, typing, etc.
O Logic and critical thinking.

These lists are fairly conservative and classical. You will no doubt add to the list and you may delete some of the items. These are personal family decisions, have the confidence to make them. Go back to your goal sheet occasionally to see the "big picture."

Hobbies and projects: The lists above are important things, but another very important subject to cover well is the subject your child is interested in studying, whatever that is at the moment. Gifted children may bounce around, studying many different topics, but these hobbies, projects, and interests have a way of becoming careers. It is good to seriously approach these topics, just as you would the normal school subjects. This does not mean you have to figure out computer programming or the new names of dinosaurs. Let kids learn what they're interested in and then show it to you, or demonstrate it, or explain it. But you don't have to learn it all yourself (unless you want to, of course!).

In seminars, we've been asked by moms questions on interest studies with gifted children. Their children seem to change interests frequently. This is normal for gifted children, but can be a problem for an energetic mom. As soon as the child mentions a new topic, she immediately hits the library to build a unit study - collecting years' worth of ideas and great activities, materials for bulletin boards, stationary, things to eat, and more. But by the time she gets home from the library, junior is on to something else. This mom needs to give her child time for independent exploration. She should encourage the interest, then sit back and appreciate what he's learning. <u>Not everything has to be planned.</u>

Other ideas to consider while planning:

❖ Gifted children come in many different sizes, each different from the next. In like manner, each will need a different kind of plan for schooling, and each will learn in unique ways. Some children will need organization. Others will astonish their parents with the speed at which they learn. Some will be able to see something once and understand it; others will require repetition. Some differences are related to the level of giftedness (as in profoundly gifted, highly gifted, and moderately gifted), but other differences will remain unexplained. Because of these differences, you may have need of a totally unorganized curriculum, or one in which your child speeds through texts without need of a regular plan. On the other hand, your child may need the organization of a schedule and a timer. Whatever the reason for the differences or the methods you choose to meet those differences, the best advice is to remain flexible, observant, and focused.

❖ Introduce evolution to your high schoolers. They need to know what it is, the facts it's founded on, and how it would, if true, affect other topics. This is a little controversial, but your high school student needs to know this subject, right or wrong. In college, many courses are based on the idea that evolution is fact. Your child should be able to write exams regurgitating that idea (perhaps neither agreeing nor disagreeing). Understanding a concept and writing it on a test does not indicate belief. As well, the evolution-creation issue should not be a challenge to his faith when he gets to university and hears something new.

❖Teach the foundational worldviews.

❖ Let your elementary students run through the Building Thinking Skills series. These books have been shown to improve thinking skills and test scores. There are actually five books: primary, Volumes 1 & 2, Volume 3 - Figural, and Volume 3 - Verbal. You can probably go right to Volume 2 and then do both of Volume 3. (7)

❖ Teach the Critical Thinking series to your junior high schooler and above. (8)

❖ Teach skills they may not learn in regular school or with standard curriculum:
> ❶ Speech making.
> ❷ Memorizing.
> ❸ Writing outlines and essays.
> ❹ Note taking from a lecture or sermon.
> ❺ How to study: this is learned when the child NEEDS to study. Seriously challenge them occasionally in school.
> ❻ How to work: or "sweat is your friend!"

These lists are intended to help plan and they aren't written in stone. Every family and student is unique and will have different needs.

Resources & Notes

1) Bright Ideas Press
See Appendix A.

www.BrightIdeasPress.com

2) Welliver, Hilary, (1998). *The Scientist's Apprentice*
Complete one-year science curriculum for K - 6, all learning styles.
Available from Bright Ideas Press. See note (1).

3) Tolman, Marvin, (1995). *Hands-on Earth Science*
A great experiment book.

Parker Publishing Co.
West Nyack, NY 10994

3) Cohen, Don, (1993) The Mathman. *Calculus for Young People,*
The Mathman
809 Stratford Drive
Champaign, IL 61821-4140
(217) 356-4555

4) Castle Heights Press, specializing in home school science resources very appropriate for gifted students. See Appendix A.
www.flash.net/~wx3o/chp

5) Critical Thinking Press, Inc.
See Appendix A.

6) See note (1).

7 and 8) See note (5).

Chapter Eight
Curriculum Considerations

Curriculum Considerations

"Results! Why, man, I have gotten a lot of results. I know several thousand things that won't work."

- Thomas Edison

You may have turned to this chapter first, looking desperately for the once-and-for-all, final, perfect curriculum for your child. Sorry to say, there is no "perfect" curriculum. There are, however, many excellent resources available that will enable you to put together an outstanding educational package for your child. We are going to discuss curriculum choices from several perspectives so that making these decisions will not seem overwhelming. First, we will cover what to look for in a curriculum designed for gifted children. The second important thing to consider is the usability of a curriculum and any special needs you may have in your family. Finally, we will discuss your specific planning.

What to Teach, When

Researchers from Johns Hopkins University say:
> "Both educational acceleration and educational enrichment constitute powerful tools in the **inevitably eclectic** plan that should be **tailored specially for each precocious child and revised continually** to accord with developing abilities, potentialities, and achievements." {Emphasis ours.} (1)

Sure sounds a lot like homeschooling, doesn't it? As you can see, their conclusions point directly to the fact that there is no one perfect resource to use, and that you will continually need to adjust your plan to meet each child's specific individual needs. Is it easy? No. Possible? Absolutely!

A curriculum for gifted children? Unfortunately, there are no whole curricula written for gifted children, and the few materials on the market were designed for an entire classroom of children. However, the situation is not as bad as it sounds, because there are many great things on the market designed for homeschoolers and independent learners.

Joyce VanTassel-Baska has pointed out four qualities of a curriculum for the gifted. (2)

- Appropriate level
- Pace
- Complexity
- Depth

If we add a few other qualities to look for in a curriculum to meet the needs of our children, we can recognize good curriculum by these characteristics:

▲ **Challenging**: both in level and in pace.

▲ Encourages **higher order thinking** skills.

▲ At least some activities which are **open-ended**, allowing the child to pursue them as deeply as he or she wants.

▲ Some questions without answers but which allow for the **expression** of the student's own ideas.

▲ Units which are **balanced in types of learning**: rote-memory, creativity, and analytical thinking.

▲ Materials which allow them to pursue subjects that **capture the imagination** and allow minds to soar. This concept is good for all students, but for the gifted child, the sort of activities we refer to may require the child to think in ways or of things they have never thought before.

At a recent conference we spoke to a woman who was shopping at our booth for gifts to bring home to each of her three children. She found things quickly for her oldest and youngest, but was stymied on a choice for her 8-year-old. "What does he like?" we asked. "I don't know," she said. "It's so hard to tell with him. He's very different from my other two." A colorful cloud chart with forecasting rules caught her eye and she decided on a whim that it might appeal to him.

The next day she came over to tell us a remarkable story. She had given each child their present that night. Her son had fallen in love with the cloud chart and insisted on sleeping with it. She was amazed that she had picked out something that this "different" child loved so much. "I told him it had been hard for me to pick something out for him. His brother and sister were easy because they both had particular collections. What do you collect?" I asked, planning to file his answer away for future reference." "I collect ideas," he said.

After discussing this child for a few minutes, I asked the woman if it had ever occurred to her that maybe her son was gifted. She said it had, but that the idea had frightened her. She made sure to keep him on grade level in his workbooks so he wouldn't pass his older brother. After seeing the effect the cloud chart had on this child, she realized it was time to let him soar. - Maggie

▲ Activities or questions which require that the child think **globally, or of broad, overarching concepts**. They should be challenging in complexity.

▲Math curriculum should have many **opportunities for problem-solving**.

▲ **Does not spend extra time on "skill building,"** as in "reading skills" or "math readiness skills." Perhaps they are available but not as a part of the main curriculum, and so can be easily bypassed.

▲ **Large print is good for small children** who can think well, but should not have to stress their eyes.

▲ **Workbooks which have large spaces** to write in are better for young children whose fine motor skills are not quite ready for smaller spaces.

▲ **Materials which don't rely on serial methods** to slowly teach concepts over several years.

Important Note One: Gifted children may find some of these characteristics very challenging because their natural bent may be towards detail rather than overarching concepts, or perhaps they're very used to the rote-memory type of text. A friend many years ago said that "if the shoe fits, it hurts." A gifted child who has never been required to think up new and creative solutions to a problem may protest; loudly, but the training is good for him. The things listed above are good to have in your curriculum, precisely because they will stretch children.

Important Note Two: Do not be deceived by the use of the words "text" or "curriculum." In a well-functioning homeschool, you'll find yourself using all sorts of materials, including texts written for adults, books written for the hobbyist or expert, computer programs, oral interviews with experts, materials from the government, 4-H, the Red Cross, and more. Any and all of these have been used by homeschoolers.

Curriculum: Usability

It's fine to talk about curriculum for gifted children, but in the end **we must be able to use whatever we choose.** So, what are some characteristics of a good, solid curriculum which make it usable for homeschooling a gifted child? The usability of a curriculum is perhaps the one most important characteristic to look for, simply because an unused book is without value. When you are choosing between several curricula and trying to determine a text's usability, ask yourself the following questions:

✐Does it help you achieve balance between ease of use, preparation time, involvement (your involvement)?

✐ Does your overall plan have a balance between structured and unstructured time based upon your philosophy, your life-style, and the learning style of your student?

✐ Is it a tutorial or dialoging method? This method is easy to use, but does it reflect higher order thinking skill?

✐ Does the material give your child some academic freedom?

✐ Is the style and sequence easy to compact? Is it well organized and systematic? Does it have pretesting or tests you can use as pretests?

✐ Do the science and history books have excellent and plentiful pictures and diagrams?

✐ Is the science or history text primarily a reader or does it focus on overarching concepts? Some elementary texts are readers; that is, books teaching easy science or history but basically designed for reading practice. Your child will learn more if a higher level text is used even if it is read to him or her.

Curriculum should meet your child's needs. Consider the following:

✔ For the "hate-to-write" student: Does the curriculum have the problems written out already?

✔ For the visual learner: Does the book have all black and white ink or does it use color? Is it arranged in a pleasing way?

✔ For the auditory learner: Are tapes available?

✔ For the young learner: Is the print large enough so that your little one does not strain his eyes?

✔ For the easily distracted learner: Does the curriculum use workbooks? Does the workbook have tear out pages so he can do one at a time? Are the pages calming, or are they very "busy" and cluttered?

✔ For the insecure parent: Is there a plan? Are there answers?

Summary: The best texts we've used have been systematic, visually pleasing, and have a well organized approach to information about the topic. These are the ones which we can supplement if required, skip around in as necessary, and use to build a good, individualized course.

Building Your Own Curriculum Plan

Writing a plan for your own student requires that you know something about the child, that you know something about his learning styles and/or needs, and that you know something about the choices you have. Take one step at a time. First, you will build an overall outline of levels and topics which means that you will research your own student first. Then you will consider any special learning needs he or she has. To do this you merely need to think about the learning characteristics of the child. Finally, you will need to make specific curriculum choices. To do this you will need information about different options. At the end of the chapter, you will find a list of resources which have reviews of the various curricula on the market.

An overall plan: Begin with the testing results for each of your students, or at least with your own knowledge of your child's functioning level. To do this, take out the records of past work, some achievement testing results, and dust off the psychological testing summary if you have it. Consider the scores together with your own goals and thoughts on his needs and rough out a plan. Here is an example of how this might look for a gifted child of eight:

Johnny can spell almost anything, especially most elementary words. He reads anything up to late high school level, including some things his mom would just as soon he not read. He can print reasonably well and only needs practice, whereas he doesn't need to do cursive for a couple of years yet. Mom has decided, based upon his testing scores, that he'll skip spelling, reading, and handwriting this year. Mom wants him to read some good books, so she jots down a list of books she and Dad remember and she will add more later on as she does more research. She decides to cover world history, composition, a little grammar, a lot of science (he has been begging for more), and math; this is a rough beginning.

You can see that Johnny's mom has thought a lot about what to do next year and that she has a pretty good plan going. She's forgotten about her overall goals, though. You cannot see her planning notebook, but one of the reasons she and her husband have decided to homeschool is so that Johnny can spend time at his grandpa's workshop. Grandpa, who is a fisherman, builds fishing rods and things. In addition, Grandpa has many stories from the past which reflect his wisdom and knowledge gained through the years. The opportunity is too good to pass up.

Johnny's mom, upon consultation with his dad, decides that the world history Johnny covers should be spiced up with Grandpa's stories. She plans to have Johnny tape them and transcribe them onto paper (practicing his typing skills, too) and put them into a book which can later be copied for other family members. Johnny will spend one day a week working at Grandpa's shop while taping the stories. He will study the habitats, habits, and anatomy of fish, too. It is not all of the science Johnny will cover this year, but it is a good start.

The other subjects Johnny will be studying, like math, will need to be slightly compacted to allow for the day spent with Grandpa. She will figure out how to do this when she looks at the math curriculum choices she has at the book fair. She does know that he will be working on math facts (his test scores were a bit low in that area) and multiplication. Perhaps a fourth grade text will do the trick.

Johnny's mom has now got a good plan started even though she does not know the specific texts or materials she will be using. She has used her families' original goals, Johnny's test results, the observational information about Johnny's abilities, and her knowledge of available resources (i.e. Grandpa) to create a plan. Now, she is ready to look at specific curriculum.

Specific needs: There are different ways to look at learning styles, but basically, this means any of the external or internal characteristics of your child which would affect learning. Evaluate your child's learning style and your own teaching style. Learning styles are particularly important to take into consideration with the gifted, because with these children, everything seems to be taken to the extreme. One child may love working his way through workbooks at an accelerated pace. Another may loathe workbooks and need to have his hands actively involved. Does he need quiet? Does she need a certain type of lighting? Does he learn best orally or visually? Read and think about these variables. You do not have to be an expert to do this. Consider your own past. What worked for you or your husband? While your child won't necessarily be like you, you can learn to judge methods by your own experience. What do you know about your own learning styles? How should it have been different for you? In what ways was school a success? When you realize you could have skipped a grade in math, or should have used an activity-driven curriculum, you're using your own life as a guide. Then, by the time you're ready to judge methods for your own children, you have had the experience of evaluating curricula for two others, you and your husband. Multiply this by talking to others about their experiences, whether their own or their children's. Interestingly, the styles of teaching in the thirties were similar to the activity-driven and hands-on approaches being used today, so you can ask your parents or grandparents about their experiences, too. (3)

Don't forget your own experience teaching your children. Even if you have never homeschooled before, you certainly have taught your children. Make notes on things you've tried in the past, whether as a parent or as a teacher. Which projects, activities, lessons, were successful? Why? Which ones bombed? Why? This will take some time, but the more time spent in the planning stage, the less time spent changing curriculum midstream.

Curriculum Options: There are a few concepts about textbooks which may affect your decisions. Let's go over a few of these characteristics with respect to arithmetic curricula. By doing so, you can learn identify them in other subjects as well. Consider these and apply them to the texts you'll be looking for at the book fair.

Conceptual bias: Texts have different ways in which they treat concepts. For example, one text may lead your child to the concept of the problem while another will focus on techniques and correct answers. (By the way, neither technique is more or less valid than the other as children really need both.)

Visual presentation: The visual presentation of a book is important, especially to a visually-oriented child. Two math books may be equal in terms of concepts covered, but one may use color throughout and visual cues to set off portions of text. This may be appealing or distracting.

Organization: The organization of a math book is very important, also. The Saxon books don't go through the domain of arithmetic in traditional order, but instead meet the objectives out of order. This can be confusing to some gifted children who experience difficulty without a systematic approach. This is especially true for global thinkers; those who learn entire concepts at once instead of sequentially (in small steps). A child like this may be happier with a more traditionally organized book. Good examples of non-spiral, traditionally organized books are: *Schaum's Outline text on Mathematics*, Farmer's *Mastering Mathematics*, and Ray's *Arithmetics*. (4)

Product reviews: For ideas about options and resources, turn to the curriculum reviews by Cathy Duffy, Mary Pride, and others. (5) Duffy's books are especially good for information about learning styles. Read their reviews and opinions of products. Resist the urge to feel overwhelmed at the number of possibilities, and take heart. There are many products out there, and none of them will damage your child. Even a bad choice can be used well (and we have all made some bad choices). Each text or set of materials was designed to achieve a set of goals. Try to figure these out from the write-ups (not always possible). If you have them, examine the reviews and assess whether the product's objective matches yours or your child's.

Attend curriculum fairs: On the first day of a curriculum fair, concentrate on learning about the materials there. Speak to the authors if possible, and definitely talk with past users. Buy the tapes if you want to hear a speaker and spend your time instead in the exhibition hall. Next year, you can take the time to go to the workshops, but this year (unless there is a very important topic on the schedule), try to stick to this plan. On your second day, you may decide to start buying. **Warning:** It's easy to feel overwhelmed at a fair, but take time, relax, have a cool drink break to think about your family's needs, and enjoy the event. A good idea is to take the map of the exhibit hall and actually cross off those booths which sell products you will not use. This will help you focus. We who regularly have booths at fairs have observed many new homeschoolers who walk by with a dazed expression! They're probably not getting much accomplished, even though they'll be exhausted by the end of the weekend. Arm yourself with your plan, a map, and focus on your own needs. And remember, concentrate on the curriculum booths, not the craft, grocery store, t-shirts, etc. - at least on the first day. Later, after you've made your curriculum choices, go back and get that special bread pan you made yourself pass by!

Note: In the homeschool arena, there are certain curricula which "everybody" uses. Don't fall into that bandwagon trap, just evaluate each curriculum according to the needs of your family. Choose wisely.

> Honestly evaluate the amount of time you have for planning and implementing curriculum. If your personality or life-style isn't suited to it, it won't work!

By now, you know a lot about learning styles, teaching styles (at least you've given thought to what you feel comfortable using), and about where your child is academically and developmentally. You've a pretty good idea of the different curricula available, and some you've actually seen and paged through at a convention. You may not think so, but you already know a lot!

Feeling overwhelmed? Check out the *Ultimate Guide to Homeschooling* by Debra Bell. It will hold your hand and walk you through the entire process. (6)

Good job! You have an overall plan for each child, you have a list of curricula or materials you will use this year, and you have even purchased a few of them already. Before you build a schedule for your year at home, you'll need to get some idea of how you're going to integrate your home schedules with the schooling schedules. Here are a few things to consider before planning your yearly schedule:

○ Balance your schedule with outside activities, hands-on materials, traditional texts or workbooks, games and the rest. If you try to do everything in unit studies, you may not be able to get the laundry done, not to mention meals, because some unit studies are "mommy-intensive." On the other hand, traditional texts can be boring and repetitive, and to spend all day in front of a video curriculum, well....you get the picture.

○ If you have a preschooler or two (or more!), you may want a pre-planned school, not a constantly changing one (usually called a "canned curriculum"). You may at least want a few subjects your child can work on independently. We know moms who use video schools because they have many children and literally do not have the time to teach each child individually. While others may criticize this, we do not because these moms know best the specific limitations of their own households.

○ Some gifted children have difficulty working independently and need constant reinforcement. They may need attention in order to stay on track. Whatever the reason, these children can upset your plans for learning independence. You may find that you can use a curriculum which is student-centered, if you stay in the room and occasionally interject commentary, keeping him on track and letting him know you're paying attention. It can be difficult to stay tied to the schoolroom, but the reward is a student who learns to work independently. **Note:** some homeschoolers criticize a super-organized homeschool, calling it "school at home," not realizing that this student may need the organization.

O Your time may be limited by many things - take this into account. For example, a kinesthetic child may require much hands-on work with Mom which takes time and energy. Because both are limited, Mom might use intensive hands-on work only for the subject in which the child is behind. For the other subjects, she may use some activities but not intensively. So, Sam who is behind in math, ahead in reading and history, and on grade level in science may do well with a hands-on math curriculum, a quality history/reading list, and a science text doing experiments/projects on a weekly or bimonthly basis. By applying a hands-on approach only where needed, you free up time and resources.

O How old is your child? For many people, elementary school and junior high is the time to be more creative and spontaneous in chosen curriculum. High school tends to become a time of traditional approaches and record keeping. Depending upon the laws concerning homeschooling in your state, evaluate exactly what must be taught and how structured or flexible you can be.

O Remember your long term goals. Knowing she'll use textbooks in the eighth grade may allow a conservative parent to feel free to try unit studies or other imaginative approaches to education in earlier grades. Even within traditional curriculum, there's room for choice.

O One of the best methods for choosing curriculum is to take your child's interests into account. A budding scientist? Go all out one year with a bang-up science program. (Go a little lighter on history or English that year.) Give her the chance to delve deeply into exciting topics and create opportunities that won't just become precious memories, but may help her focus on specific, lifelong career goals.

It may seem overwhelming at first to narrow down the choices for each particular student and year. Some parents tend to over-buy, while others become frozen with indecision.

Relax, love them, and they will learn! No curriculum will ever take the place of your love and support. A less than successful curriculum choice one year simply means you'll be better prepared to choose next year's. Allow yourself the freedom to make a mistake in curriculum. And really, no curriculum is bad, some are just better for your situation than others.

Resources & Notes

1) Johns Hopkins University
> 3400 North Charles Street
> Baltimore, MD 21218
> (410) 516-0277
> www.jhu.edu/gifted

2) Joyce VanTassel-Baska, (1996). *Excellence in Educating Gifted & Talented Learners*, ISBN 0-89108-255-7
> Love Publishing Company
> Denver, CO 80222

3) Tobias, Cynthia, (199_). *The Way We Learn.*
I'm an abstract random. My husband is a concrete sequential. I wish I'd known this years ago! We understand each other a lot more now after discovering Tobias' interesting, humorous, and practical explanations of learning styles. - Maggie

4) Farmer, Letz, (1988) *Mastering Mathematics and Mathematics Skill Inventory*
> Mastery Publications
> 90 Hillside Lane
> Arden, NC 28704-9709
> (828) 684-0429

5) Reviewers:
Duffy, Cathy, (1997). *The Christian Home Educators' Curriculum Manual.* Two books, one for elementary and the other for junior/senior high school. Updated regularly and widely available. Excellent chapters on "How to Choose Curriculum," which includes a thorough explanation of learning styles and how to determine which curriculum matches various styles. Comprehensive reviews of a variety of homeschooling materials.

Pride, Mary, (1987). *The Big Book of Home Learning.* Widely thought to be the standard in home education material reviews. Mary pulls no punches in giving you her honest opinion. Written from a Christian world view. Also updated regularly. (Revised 2000.)

6) Bell, Debra, (1997). *The Ultimate Guide to Homeschooling.* "An on-ramp to a powerful new way to educate your children and maximize your family life. ...sets forth a compelling vision for the joys of home-based learning and the essential tools for success."

Question:
What frustrates you?

Answers:
All the book work that's boring.
- Laura Reisinger, age 9

Being serious, filling out forms, doing one thing for very long, writing by hand...
-JB Hogan, age 14 (While filling out this questionnaire.☺)

People talking to me when I work.
-Benjamin Winston, age 6

Chapter Nine
Techniques We Can Use

When families take gifted children out of regular school, as they are doing in increasing numbers, they face many of the same problems that teachers of the gifted face in school. The rates at which our children learn, the asynchronies, and even learning disabilities are all still there. In this chapter we'll cover some ideas and educational techniques you can use with your gifted children, covering such topics as crisis management, detox periods, subjects, compacting, teaching several children, and block scheduling. Feel free to be choosy. Adapt at will.

Coming out of a crisis situation? Or just starting out? Many gifted children are leaving the regular schools not because of a philosophical predilection for homeschooling but because of a crisis situation at school. Often, the child may have behavioral or psychological problems associated with schooling difficulties. As well, many parents are simply tired of the rat race of dealing with the schools. So, relax for a time. Let your child detox from regular school for at least three months (summer vacation does not count). Perhaps the whole family needs some time off. Let your student do some projects. Occasionally, a student will not be interested in doing anything. This attitude is a product of the school environment and will usually fade after a few months. You may have to assign work, but make it as free-wheeling and as different from regular school as it can reasonably be. Lots of drawing and field trips, hiking, reading (no book reports), planning trips, and camping are a few ideas.

Fill the holes: Any student coming home from regular school will have holes in her training. Expect 'em, find 'em, and fill 'em. Recently, at a convention in a western state, we were informed that children are not taught their math facts in the local schools. Schools not teaching the multiplication tables? Sounds like heresy, but that kind of thing is going on all over the United States.

Get a physical: If your child shows signs of reading difficulty or a similar problem, please get it checked. Some homeschoolers, in a very well-meaning way, have been known to advise moms to "just wait, he'll grow out of it." Vision and hearing problems rarely just "go away," and they may get worse with the extra waiting. Get it checked.

Re-mediate disabilities: Cure or cope: whatever your philosophy, do it. By the way, for a gifted child, an average score in a WISC subarea may be considered a sign of a disability. What you do with a disability is up for grabs. Some specialists think a learning disability is permanent, and the student must learn to cope with it. Others believe it a problem that can be cured. We personally believe a two-pronged attack is best: try for the cure, but teach him to cope. Whatever your personal approach, don't neglect the problem. (1)

Don't know the answer? Ask the experts: This is good advice when you're stumped about how to teach something you don't know a lot about. If you don't feel confident in foreign languages, ask the experts. In other areas, in which you feel more confident, ask the experts and then decide whether it makes sense or not. Check with the experts no matter what the subject area, then have the courage to make your own opinions.

Reading: With an advanced reader, test for reading skills and leave reading behind. Most "reading skills" are intuitive for good readers.

Mathematics: For the young mathematician, use the prescriptive method used by Johns Hopkins University. You don't have to use all (or any) manipulatives with a child who is intuitive in math.

Science: Discard the idea that science is the big three: biology, chemistry, and physics. Forget age-level science texts for your elementary student, reading to them instead from higher level books and books with good pictures. In addition to science studies, let them "play" with science: electronics kits, toys like Erector™ sets and Legos™, Toys in Space™ videos from NASA, rocketry, and collecting rocks. These are only some of the ideas you can use. Teach the skills of science: observing, recording, measuring, drawing, and line charting while doing your experiments. (2, 3)

Grammar: Don't do grammar every year or even every other year, unless they struggle with it. Use a non-spiral method technique. You probably don't need manipulatives for grammar, or songs, or games, unless their particular learning style would greatly benefit from them.

Compacting and Telescoping Courses

Acceleration is a good thing for gifted students. This means the rapid progression through a course, or the entire skipping of a course or grade. To help you decide about acceleration, see Chapter Ten.

The key to doing acceleration well is **using the objectives of the curriculum**. All curriculum is based on educational objectives. Sometimes, the objectives are actually written in the text, but most of the time, they're on the author's notepad, unknown to us. You can read the table of contents of a math text and understand many of the objectives. You can read the text itself and put together an outline which will show the objectives. If you know the objectives of the author, you can easily decide whether his/her materials fit your goals. You can also use the textbook more creatively, such as for telescoping or compacting. Some ideas for using objectives include:

❑ In the last part of a pre-algebra text, chapter headings will include some of these concepts: single variable equations, slope, graphing equations, and factoring. Look into the table of contents of an Algebra I book and you'll see some of the same chapter headings. The concepts are usually exactly the same in each case. An excellent way to accelerate your student is to skip those chapters in the pre-algebra text, and in so doing, choose to learn those concepts while studying the Algebra I text. The student hasn't lost a thing! This can be done with Algebra I and Algebra II. In the normal case, these two courses are taught two years apart with geometry between, resulting in a real need for review of basic algebra concepts. If your student takes geometry and Algebra II at the same time, she'll be able to skip all of the review (usually four or five chapters). Of course, if you do have geometry and Algebra II at the same time, you'll need to drop another course, perhaps history. Likewise, there are similar chapters or topics taught in both chemistry and physics; the gas laws, for example.

❑ If you'd like to give your children an introduction to chemistry or physics, choose the high school level text, not physical science, a junior high course. Start them out on the first four or five chapters of the chemistry or physics text. Later, when you get to high school and wish to study them in more detail, just do a quick review of the material and skip right on to chapter six or whichever one is next.

> *When Joseph and Esther were at home for tenth grade, we did biology, but because they both intended to major in engineering, we decided to do a science spring. That spring, they covered five chapters of physics and six of chemistry, while finishing up biology. Later on, they were able to skip to appropriate places in their texts, a benefit which allowed them to finish the books well and still have time for lab. Of course, they did not take history or grammar that spring. - Kathleen*

❑ While looking at the objectives in elementary English, you'll see the similarity between years. Why not combine years, fulfill the higher level objectives, and move on?

❑American history is something which can be compacted. The CTY people at Johns Hopkins are able to get it all into three weeks, a seemingly unbelievable feat until we remember the hours. A normal high school course meets about 180 days for about 50 minutes. Even though we know all that time isn't spent working on history, that comes out to 150 hours on task. At a rate of eight hours per day, you can still do it in approximately nineteen days, less than four weeks! At Johns Hopkins, American history was compacted in time, but all objectives were accomplished and they included field trips. You can do this, too.

❑ American history is commonly taught many times throughout the twelve years, especially in elementary school. In the last ten years many new curriculum materials have been offered to homeschoolers, much of which we can't use because our time has been stolen by too much reliance upon regular school texts which would have your child going over and over the same material. Instead, make a list of the things you would like to accomplish. Then choose curriculum which meets your goals, compacting and skipping to make time for new material. In this way, you can prepare a set with little overlap and repetition. One year you can work on pioneer skills and discovery stories upon which so much of our American spirit is based, while covering the details (names and dates) later on, and the theory of democracy still later. By not doing names and dates every year, you'll leave lots of room for fun stuff and overarching principles.

❑ Another good way to compact a study and save or make up time is to do a subject orally. It's surprising how much ground you can cover that way! We often did Latin II this way, since so much of it is translation. Caesar is more fun, too, when you do his books as a family, each taking a sentence to translate aloud.

❑ Probably the most classic way of compacting "on the run" is through the pretest. If your student can do the work, then skip the lessons. Try this first with spelling and vocabulary. Have your student spell aloud or on paper through successive lessons until he misses twenty or thirty. These then will be his list for the week. Note: if your child only misses one word out of twenty, forget spelling all together. She's going to pick up the ones she doesn't know easily enough. We have also noticed that some children can spell accurately aloud, but not on paper. Check both ways with your child if you are in doubt about his spelling.

❏If you don't have an easy way to pretest, then use the tests at the end of the chapter as pretest material. If all else fails, use the actual test.

❏ Saxon texts may be difficult since there are no pretests, but there is a way. Have your mathematically gifted student read over five lessons at one session, do a few practice problems, and take the test (ten lessons behind where he's working). In one day he may be able to go through five lessons. Some children do this easily, and when they start missing an inappropriate number of problems (concept, not carelessness), then they can slow down and take it at a different pace. This is especially useful if you're pulling a child out of regular school where he had a different text. As well, you can also do just the odds or even in Saxon, although the publisher doesn't recommend it. For more information on compacting go to Chapter Ten.

Teaching several children: There are helpful hints to homeschooling with several levels of children at once. But in fact, homeschooling mothers with preschoolers should be given awards for endurance! Here are a few tips which were passed on to us years ago. They work very well with gifted children.

▶ Teach phonics while the older kids are working independently.

▶Don't try to teach two levels of math at the same time of the day to different children unless you're really good at thinking on your feet.

▶Teach history together with languages like Latin to all of your school-age children. There are many texts at different levels which can be used together.

▶ Teach science and history topics on a three or four year rotation. Kids who are in third grade and above can dissect together. For example:
>   Year 1: Biology (or life sciences) & biological sciences.
>   Year 2: Chemistry or foundational sciences.
>   Year 3: Geology or Earth Science.
>   Year 4: Physics or physical sciences (like electronics, etc.).
>   Year 5: Random or start over (not repeating material, just topics).

▶Use the same grammar series and teach all of the children together. Those in the same series generally proceed on the same schedule.

▶Use a timer to keep on schedule even if your best friend says that it's too regimented. You know your needs best. You'll get more done and have more freedom to have fun.

▶If you feel the need for a tight schedule, use one. Homeschoolers have peer pressures, too, and you don't have to submit to those pressures.

▶ Sometimes look the other way when the younger ones listen in on the older ones' discussions. They do learn a lot that way, even if their current work isn't completed.

▶Use protector pages on books like the Building Thinking Skills series. The kids can use overhead projector markers which will just wash off afterward, leaving the page clear and ready for the next child.

This chapter has listed a number of helps, techniques, and advice which we have learned over the years. Read them over, think about them, and use what you need. Because we all have children who are so different, you may have to invent your own answers to certain problems. Write and tell us about your solutions.

Have the confidence to be innovative. You can successfully teach your child at home!

Question:
Do you have any advice for parents teaching smart children at home?

Answers:
Do not let your kids put off things like me. Teach them the rewards of _diligence_!
- Susanna Shipman, age 11

Never over or underestimate their abilities.
- Kirsten Winston, age 11

Resources & Notes

1) Educators Publishing Service, Inc. sells many excellent materials for children with learning disabilities.

31 Smith Place
Cambridge, MA 02138-1089
(800) 435-7728
www.epsbooks.com

Trudy Palmer publishes wonderful materials for reading problems, as well as auditory discrimination materials. *The Gift of Reading and In One Ear and (Hopefully Not) Out the Other* (1995).

Homeschool Instructional Services
423 Maplewood Lane
San Antonio, TX 78216-6848

Critical Thinking Press has a new book with activities for the early student in visual spacial perception. Raya Bursten, (1998). Visual-Spatial Perception. See Appendix B.

Materials concerning the visual-spatial learner can be purchased from:
Gifted Development Center in Denver.
1452 Marion Street
Denver, CO 80218
Phone: (303) 837-8378
Fax: (303) 837-7465
www.gifteddevelopment.com

2) Castle Heights Press
www.flash.net/~wx3o/chp
See Appendix B.

3) Bright Ideas Press
www.BrightIdeasPress.com
See Appendix B.

Question:
What frustrates you?

Answers:
Math and spelling m o s t y. (sic)
-Susanna Shipman, age 11

When Matthew finds a new interest, such as CIV (computer game), sports, reading a certain series of books, etc., he lives, breathes, and sleeps it for two or more weeks. He does this until all the facts are fully absorbed.
-Jean, mother of Matthew, age 11

Chapter Ten
Acceleration and Grade Skipping

One question we're often asked is "Should my child skip a grade?" In response we say there are many different ramifications to consider. Certainly, not every gifted child needs to be moved ahead, but if you're thinking about acceleration, first let's define the terms:

Acceleration: Moving through curriculum at a faster rate. This may be done by compacting, telescoping, and skipping, or some combination of these techniques.

Telescoping: Completing all work for a grade or a subject in less than the usual time required.

Compacting: Completing a subject in less than the usual time required by reducing the amount of work required, but not the required concepts.

Skipping (or radical acceleration): Literally not completing work for a given year; i.e., going directly from second to fourth grade.

Johns Hopkins University has done significant research into acceleration issues through the Center for Talented Youth. Check out their research which is very favorable to skipping gifted children ahead in school. (1) We highly recommend checking with a reputable homeschool support group within your state to see if there are any restrictions or guidelines for accomplishing your plan to accelerate or skip. Let's go over some of the advantages and disadvantages to acceleration, our personal experiences with acceleration, and a review of some of the things you should consider about acceleration.

ADVANTAGES TO ACCELERATION
✦ The child can work at her own pace. (No "Sorry, you're too young to read," or "You have to wait until third grade before you can do fractions.")

✦ It frees a parent to look at the individual child's needs rather than what's expected in such and such a grade.

✦ Acceleration allows parents to give a child the freedom to move ahead where strong, and to go slower in other areas. (For example, your strong reader may be on a fifth grade level in English and third in math.)

✛ Your school year can be much more flexible than the typical start in September, end in June school year, although you may still choose to do that.

DISADVANTAGES TO ACCELERATION

✛ It may confuse your child or in-laws when you're asked the inevitable "What grade are you in?" question.

✛ It may cause confusion when registering for programs that enroll by grade level.

✛ Everything isn't as neat and tidy. It can be difficult throwing out traditional mind-sets about grades and school years.

✛ Some curriculum is intertwined in its treatment of subjects. For example, one publisher's seventh grade curriculum for history, English, and science may all be (more or less) written around Ancient Civilizations. Many see this as an advantage, but if your child is ahead in science, but behind in English, using this curriculum may not work.

✛ It may be difficult starting school in September to finish the last half of a grade. For instance, concepts may need review before going on to the second half of the material after a long, summer break. In textbooks, such reviews are typically built into the beginning of the year.

ADVANTAGES TO SKIPPING A GRADE

✛ You may allow your child to work at his ability and yet remain in the mainstream by starting a new grade each September, even though the new year's work may be at a different level. This partially eliminates the need for compacting. Note: the higher the level of giftedness, the more likely that regular course work and pacing even if at a higher level will not be enough intervention.

✛ For children who are equally advanced in most, if not all, subject matter, and for those who are emotionally mature, this may be just the right solution.

✛ For those all-around bright children, much time is saved by skipping a grade that would basically be review for them.

✛ Skipping a grade within the home is a much simpler process than skipping in a traditional school setting.

✛ You save a year's worth of time and curriculum.

DISADVANTAGES TO SKIPPING A GRADE

✛ It's possible that your very precocious first grader won't continue developing at that rate and will find himself feeling quite overwhelmed in the next school grade. Note: However, this is not a common problem at school, and is not a factor at home. The problems are usually connected with peer and teacher acceptance. (1)

✛ The ever-present problem of being younger in other situations: what do you do about Sunday school class and other programs that may classify the students by grade? Will you keep them with age-mates or grade-mates?

✛ What will you do with a 16-year-old who has graduated from high school, possibly before learning to drive? Will she go off to college? Work a year? Decisions made in elementary school can have new implications during the teen years, when physical development and college decisions play important roles.

✛ The "bragging" factor - teaching your child (and your family!) how to handle grade questions with heartfelt humility. Will you be able to remember that no matter how hard you try, some misunderstandings will still arise?

ACCELERATE OR SKIP? CONSIDERATIONS:

◆ Is your child emotionally mature for his or her age?
◆ Is your child physically mature for his or her age?
◆ Is your child bored with his or her current schoolwork?
◆ Are your child's friends typically older?
◆ Is your child appropriately challenged?

After you and your spouse have thought, researched, taken into account the personality and learning style of your student, and made the decision to skip or accelerate, it is time to develop a plan of action. This plan will help you feel confident in your decision and enable you to answer questions from others in a more knowledgeable manner. Answering neighbors, friends, and relatives in a loving way, backed with research and a definite action plan, will go a long way toward disarming disagreements and allaying doubts.

OTHER POINTS:

◆ Which year will we skip or accelerate? Some feel the even school years are most repetitive and that the odd years are when new materials are introduced. Look through the curriculum you're using and see if you notice this pattern. If so, an even year may be the best year to skip.
◆ Will you leave him with grade-mates in social and other settings? Only

you can answer this question, based on the knowledge of your child's needs and understanding of his maturity. If in doubt, leave him where he is to develop socially now, and move him later if necessary.

◆ The decision to skip or accelerate must be based on how your family operates, and on the pros and cons of each option.

How have we done it? Although each family's situation is unique, allow us to share our experiences.

When we began homeschooling our oldest, JB, he was starting fourth grade. We didn't have a specific plan to accelerate him, but we found we were completing things more quickly than the usual time frame. We began keeping records of "subjects completed by grade." Over the course of three years he completed four grades, and it was a gradual and painless acceleration. He began eighth grade while the age of a seventh grader. Some people thought we had skipped seventh grade, but actually, he had done all the necessary work (although maybe not all the "busy" work.) During eighth grade, he took two high school courses in addition to his eighth grade work. For ninth grade he got ambitious and took eight high school credits. (By the way, it was a stressful year and we don't recommend that heavy a course load.) He graduated at fifteen, which has its own set of advantages and disadvantages!

During this time, we kept JB with his age-mates in other activities, such as Sunday school and scouts. This worked well for us. We plan on using a similar course of action with Tyler, our youngest son, who is gifted verbally and mathematically, but who, for now, lacks the necessary fine motor skills to do some of the higher level work. (In other words - he can do the work verbally, but please don't ask him to write it down!) At least this time we have a plan, having learned through trial and error with our older son.
- Maggie

We took a different route with our son, Seth. When Seth was twelve, I had gone as far as I felt comfortable teaching him math. After completing Saxon Algebra, Seth enrolled at the local university in a freshman math course. He enjoyed the challenge and did exceedingly well. Each semester he took another course, eventually adding sciences and humanities as he got older. He used these courses as both high school and college credits. By the time he graduated from high school, he had completed almost two years of college!

Several valuable things were discovered through this process. One, always check the syllabus and textbooks for college classes. We were dismayed at some of the material, especially in the English courses. Two, Seth accrued so many credits that when he was actually ready to attend college full-time, he was no longer a freshman. We quickly found that many, if not most, scholarships are tied to incoming freshmen. This left him in the position of having to decide to give up on certain scholarships or to drop hard-earned credits in order to be classified a freshman. - Janice

Each of our children took a different route. When we enrolled Joseph and Esther in kindergarten each was the oldest in his/her kindergarten class. They were reading at fairly high levels and both doing multiplication at this point, but we never really thought about keeping them permanently out of regular school. So, in they went. By the time Joe was in fourth grade and Esther in third, it was obvious that the curricula were not enough. After testing, we determined to skip them up a grade each. When Esther hit eighth grade and Joe, ninth, we homeschooled again. We decided to blend Esther's year into a combined eighth-ninth year. This meant that not only did she and Joe have the same classes, but that they would graduate together. She took driver's education in her senior year and was admitted into Rice University at fifteen. Joseph took college classes in his senior year instead of twelfth grade material while maintaining a job selling computers and working on his Westinghouse project. Daniel and Sarah (who started school at five) went pretty much through the twelve year cycle, but because they were accelerated in subject matter though not in grades, took college course work and advanced placement classes in their later years at home. In this way they had extra time for projects, jobs, and independent studies, yet were still 17 and 18 before going away to college. Each of our children used different forms of acceleration to meet his or her specific needs. - Kathleen

If the curriculum you're using is too easy, has too much busy work, or is moving too slowly, your child may benefit from acceleration. Use compacting, telescoping or even skipping to accelerate your child until he's moving at a rate more comfortable for him. One wonderful benefit to homeschooling is that any or all of these options are certainly possible!

It's important to remember that the question of acceleration is practically a moot point for the homeschooler. Your objective is to let your child grow and develop at his or her own rate, and this means in the academic area, too.

Some problems with any type of acceleration to consider:
❖ Family and friends may not understand your dilemma. (This can be a sticky issue!)

❖ Their age at graduation (or matriculation back into the regular school twelve year cycle) may be young, perhaps even too young for going off to college.

❖ Can your child handle the usual amount of handwork required by the upper level subjects? Can you cope with this limitation?

❖It's possible than your child would stand a better chance at the National Merit Awards if he or she were older. We've noticed that every time our children took the tests their scores improved, so had they been a year or two older, the scores may have been even higher. However, the National Merit should not be the only thing you consider in this decision. After discussing options and writing down your plan, begin with confidence that you're making the best possible educational decision for your child. Even if he does not continue to progress at the same rate, there is no problem because you can review your plan on a regular basis. If, upon review, you see that it isn't working out as desired, don't despair. Just revisit the process and revise your plan as needed.

Resources & Notes

1) A useful manual with research and statistics concerning acceleration versus skipping: *College Bound.*. Available from Johns Hopkins.
CTY
Office of Public Information
2701 N. Charles Street
Baltimore, MD 21218
(410) 516-0277

2) Check out the reproducible planning pages in the back of this book. They'll help you through this process.

*"Travel is fatal
to prejudice,
bigotry and
narrow-mindedness."*

- Mark Twain

Chapter Eleven
Activities for Gifted Kids

It's important to nurture more than just the academic side, so here are suggested activities that will enhance learning while creating enjoyable experiences. Topics we cover here are travel, kids running businesses, time with dad, meaty materials, time for dreaming, special programs for gifted students, and computers. (Because the topic of computers is so extensive, we have separated it into another chapter.)

Travel

There are few better ways than travel to capture a child's interest and imagination. The possibilities are endless!

● Younger children enjoy trips to "real" places where they can see first hand how things work. A trip behind the scenes at the post office and grocery store are worth far more than books, because a child can see for himself what's involved, and because there's someone right there to whom he can ask his 101 questions!

● Family outings to zoos and museums take on a whole new meaning with planning. Questions about what to look for and meaningful discussions can turn a mediocre trip into one worth remembering. For example, before going to the natural history museum, call or write ahead and get an idea of their specialties and a map. Zone in on particular aspects your child is likely to be interested in. Create a simple worksheet or map to be filled out during or after the trip. Concentrating on one topic with specific questions will help her pay more attention and cement the information she's acquiring. A trip to the museum store for postcards, sea shells, or books on the topic will round out the experience.

TIP: Ask if they have teacher packets when contacting them. Good stuff can be gleaned from their prepared literature.

● Children benefit from trips specifically related to a subject or time period. Williamsburg, VA will mean more if something about its time period has been read and discussed before visiting. A trip to a print shop when studying communication, a candle store when learning about early American skills, or an air and space museum when reading about the history of flight will solidify concepts. Trips also provide outlets for questions and further learning about others. (1)

TIP for overachieving parents: Is it hard to imagine going somewhere interesting without turning it into an "educational field trip?" There is much value in **simply experiencing** life in other places, whether it be the big city two hours away, a first time camping trip, or even life in another country. Making the most out of your travel is commendable, but don't be obsessive! Don't insist on a report for every single trip out of town. Balance "freestyle learning" with structured education. Loosen up - ride that roller coaster instead of studying about the effects of gravity!

● Be open to various travel opportunities. Visit family and friends in other places. How about a missions trip (2), a family camp, or a conference held in a place you've never been before? There's much to be gained in the growth and maturity of a child when confronted with experiences out of the normal sphere of their daily lives.

● Host an exchange student.

> *We hosted an exchange student from Paraguay for a year. Bruno became a part of our family. After he returned to South America we kept in touch, promising JB that "one day" he could visit his new big brother. "One day" came sooner than we expected - the month of his thirteenth birthday. Bruno's parents welcomed JB into their home for an entire month. He went to school with their youngest son, traveled, ate, and spoke lots of Spanish! It was the ultimate field trip! - Maggie*

● While traveling, listen to music and story tapes and discuss them. Or use the time in the car to become familiar with foreign languages.

> *We did a lot of traveling as a military family, and we always took along books we could read aloud in the car. I'll never forget the trip we read The Hobbit. The youngsters were really enthralled with the story and hated it when I "ran down" and lost my voice. They were a little young for it, and so were a bit frightened at the scary parts but all smiles during the rest of the story. - Kathleen*

Kids Running Businesses

As all entrepreneurs know, dreaming up a business and actually implementing one are two different things. Starting and running a business will provide many avenues of learning for your gifted child. Let's look at some of the skills needed to succeed:

Brainstorming
Organization
Self-discipline
Writing a business plan, report
Leadership
Math (probably lots of it)
Communication skills

Management techniques
Marketing
Advertising
Psychology (sales)
Banking skills
Fiscal responsibility
... and so much more!

There are a number of books available on kids' businesses. Also, check out books written for adults for your high school entrepreneur. The "Guerrilla Series" have much to offer. (3)

The Small Business Administration works with local colleges to provide informative seminars and classes, as well as personal business consultation, free of charge. With our two youngest still in the house when we started a family business, I took them along to classes and asked them to participate like any other business person. Of course, it helped that they had pooled their allowance money to write and publish a book of their own: Geometric Constructions. (4) They were well treated and the instructors invariably encouraged their participation. It was a great experience. - Kathleen

Dad Time

Time spent with dad is invaluable. Let your children participate in the activities dad does, whether it be fishing, tending the garden, or working on the car. As Kathleen's husband, Mark, says repeatedly in his seminars, "Share your hobbies with your children. Besides creating memories, you could be constructing careers!"

"One father is more than one hundred schoolmasters."

- George Herbert

Mark included the kids in his amateur radio hobby and they (well, most of them) got their own tickets. Of course they brought me along, too. To improve their Morse code speed, Mark built an oscillator and set it up in the classroom. At random times during the day, I would tap out something like: "If you can translate this, go get five Oreos™ " or "take a ten minute reading-your-book break." It was really funny to see 10-year-old Sarah dashing off for her Oreos™ while 13-year-old Daniel sat looking frustrated. Mark bought them hand-held radios after they passed their exams and they carried them everywhere. Sarah's radio was especially useful when her lambs were born in the neighbor's barn across the street and she needed help quickly.

The children also participated in the rebuilding of our Taylorcraft airplane. That experience helped Esther get a summer internship at the Smithsonian Institution Air and Space Museum restoring a Hawker Hurricane. They even paid her a salary for having fun!

Through the years, Mark has led the kids through rebuilding an MG Midget, fishing, flying lessons, radio-controlled airplanes and cars, wooden models, planting gardens, building power supplies, rewiring the house, building additions on various houses, repairing appliances, becoming amateur radio operators, and installing antennas. - Kathleen

Yes, spending time with dad is rewarding time for all concerned. Homeschooling isn't just for moms!

Meaty Materials and Creative Talk

Besides taking your kids places, provide them with access to meaty materials. Good books, shows, and conversations are all components upon which a gifted child can build.

This is very significant. Talk to your children, spend time with them, value them, and be willing to go out of your way to educate them well. They're important!

Give them books to read, places to go, museums to wander through, and kits to build. Exposure to lots of activities is important, too. Give them time by not scheduling every minute of every day. We found that if we had to leave the house for any reason, the day was shot; well, not completely, but we just didn't get everything done we had planned.
Use your time wisely.

Time for Dreaming

TIP for overachieving parents: Earmark this page and read it often.

As worthwhile as trips, classes, activities, clubs, etc. may be, it's also important to allow your child some time to be, well, *a child*. Time to plan, dream, reflect, remember; things adults forget they need! Do you remember dreaming? Do you still dream? Give your child the precious gift of a reasonable amount of spare time in this busy, overcommitted world of ours, for it is through remembering and dreaming that old ideas are examined and new ideas are born. These seeds may later bear fruit in wonderful new stories, inventions, or just deeper levels of understanding; building blocks for your child to grow on.

> *When I think back to our homeschooling days, the two hour lunch breaks are the most memorable. The children could eat and then read, play instruments, build models, finish dissecting their own personal frog (Fred), or whatever they chose during that time. There were times when I would get spring fever and we would decide to just leave the house, take the drawing pencils and notebooks, unfinished math pages, and Latin we were reading, and head for the nearest park. There were the hours spent doing my sewing or whatever in the school room so that I could be near to keep young minds on task. There were the endless interesting discussions the kids started in order to get out of doing their work, but which we finished because they really were interesting.*

> *Whatever you do, we encourage you to fill your hours with the doing of things, wonderful, interesting, memorable things, not merely workbooks. My children are off now, doing the things planned for them and living their lives. Homeschooling was a challenge. It was, admittedly, boring sometimes, but it's also gone now, except for our memories. - Kathleen*

Nationally Recognized Gifted Programs

What kinds of programs are available for kids who test in the highly gifted range? The one we're most familiar with is CTY or Center for Talented Youth sponsored by Johns Hopkins University. They offer educational summer programs for qualified students grades two and up that are diverse and stimulating. Seventh graders' eligibility is determined by SAT scores and the student's age. For example, to meet their criteria for math and science courses, a student who is between 13 years and 6 months and 14 years and 0 months must have a score of greater than or equal to 540 on the Math section and a combined Math + Verbal score of greater than or equal to 1070. For Humanities courses, the score must be greater than or equal to 530 to qualify.

When Seth was 12-years-old, he qualified for the CTY program and chose to take their Writing I course. It was the first time he was away from home for a significant period of time (three weeks). He flew to Saratoga Springs, New York, for his classes at Skidmore College. At first he was homesick and thought he would give up and come home. After the first week though, he really began enjoying the challenge of his studies AND the diverse student population, all of whom were academically gifted. He received a glowing evaluation from his teacher, which was to have a significant bearing in his future goals.

Two years later, he again had the opportunity to go to CTY. This time he chose to study Logic at Franklin and Marshall College in Lancaster, Pennsylvania, much closer to our home in Delaware. Being more mature and having some idea of what to expect, he was definitely a "happy camper." They even had a debate team and Seth was chosen by his peers to be Captain. At the end of the three weeks when we went to pick him up, we had the opportunity to meet with his instructor who gave us his view not only of Seth's academic progress, but also of his social capabilities. His evaluation confirmed what we already expected, which is that homeschooling doesn't have the negative effect on social skills that so many expect. It was a rewarding experience for Seth and for us. He learned a great deal, made new friends, and had a lot of fun.

Little did we imagine just how significant these two summer sessions would be when it came time to apply for university admission and scholarship consideration. The universities Seth considered ALL offered him full tuition scholarships, and he was even awarded three college English credits based on his Writing I work at CTY, done when he was twelve! - Janice

Three of my children attended CTY classes. Daniel qualified, but we couldn't afford to send him at the time. This turned out to be unfortunate because MIT admissions (Massachusetts Institute of Technology) said they would have accepted Dan if he had gone to CTY. (Sarah loved Ireland - The next year she decided to teach herself Irish.) - Kathleen

Johns Hopkins has expanded their outreach to much younger academically talented students, currently beginning in the second grade. In addition to their summer programs, they offer workshops, symposiums, correspondence, and computer courses. Eligibility requirements vary. (5)

Remember, if your child doesn't qualify for CTY, it doesn't mean he's not gifted! This is a **high-end gifted** program - there are many different degrees of giftedness. (However, if your child tests and comes close to making it, it may be worth taking again the following year. The test itself, and the unfamiliar surroundings may be intimidating. Preparing for the test and having a better idea of what to expect the next year may be enough to pull up the test score.)

There are other Talent Searches besides CTY that are geared for finding academically talented youth in the seventh or eighth grade years. There are Talent Search programs in many regions of the world now. (6)

There are many other programs across the United States and abroad. (7) The Summer Institute for the Gifted is held at George School in PA, Bryn Mawr College in PA, Vassar College in NY, Drew University in NJ, and Oberlin College In OH. This is similar to program at Johns Hopkins, although their criteria and scope are somewhat different.

Midwest Talent Search (a function of Northwestern University, see notes) offers a booklet on summer opportunities for gifted children. Get it and plan ahead. They may be expensive, but they are worth it. Some of these programs offer scholarships and grants; ask. For many participating children, it was the first time in their lives that they were able to be among intellectual peers.

Resources & Notes

1) Yellow Pages Guide to Field Trips, published by Noble Press.

2) Missions trips: See note (7), Chapter Five.

3) Levinson, Jay and Seth Godin. *Guerilla Marketing for the Home-Based Business.* One of the many practical books in the Guerilla Marketing Series. Published by Houghton Mifflin Co.

4) Julicher, Daniel & Sarah, (1991). *Geometric Constructions.* Castle Heights Press, (800) 763-7148   www.flash.net/~wx3o/chp

5) Center for Talented Youth - CTY

Johns Hopkins University
3400 North Charles Street
Baltimore, MD 21218
(410) 516-0277
www.jhu.edu/gifted

Center for Talented Youth
Western Regional Office
The Johns Hopkins University
4640 Admiralty Way, Suite 301
Marina Del Rey, CA 90292-6613
(310) 754-4100

6)   **Duke University**
Talent Identification Program (TIP)
Box 90747
Durham, NC 27701
(919) 684-3847
www.tip.duke.edu
quarterly newsletter for parents available

Northwestern University
Center for Talent Development
617 Dartmouth Place
Evanston, IL 60208
(847) 491-3782
www.northwestern.edu

University of Denver
Center for Educational Services
Rocky Mountain Talent Search (RMTS)
2135 E. Wesley Ave.
Denver, CO 80208
(303) 871-2983
www.du.edu/education/ces/rmts.html

University of Washington
Halbert Robinson Center for the Study of Capable Youth
Box 351630
Seattle, WA 98195-1630
(206) 543-4160
www.depts.washington.edu/cscy

7) For a list of summer programs contact **College Gifted Programs**
120 Littleton Road, Suite 201
Parsippany, NJ 07054-1803
(201) 334-6691

Chapter Twelve
Computers

Ah, computers. The love, the hate, the fear they invoke! If you and your child are already computer literate, feel free to skip to the end of this chapter where we'll discuss computer uses and pitfalls. If not, read every single word - it's important. Whether you are "techno-phobic" or a "techno-wannabe," this chapter is for you.

It may not be possible for you to buy or upgrade your old computer immediately, but begin planning for it now. Your children need to become computer literate.

No Computer? Here are some ideas: For those without computers, there are still ways to get your children (and yourself) this valuable experience. Consider these options:

✍ Take a class at your local college. This may provide you with free entry to their computer lab, access to the Internet, and e-mail.

✍ Check out the public library for possible computer availability. Let the kids use the card catalog freely for research.

✍ Computer classes. These cost, but look at it as a valuable part of their education.

✍ Computer Co-op: you teach my kid computer and I'll teach yours woodworking, sewing, math, or whatever.

✍ At a minimum, begin reading computer magazines and books in order to become familiar with the terminology and technology. This will help you to become more comfortable with one when you do get the opportunity. There are several good computer magazines out for families, and at least one written for homeschooling families. (1)

The Computer is a Tool. Just like a text or a hammer, the computer is a tool for us to use. While there are some people who make a living working on computers, most simply use computers. We may not need to learn to program our PC, but we do need to use it efficiently. So, how do we give our children the opportunity to learn about computers?

Use computers for:
✓ Typing (or keyboarding as they call it now).
✓ Games that teach.
✓ Programs for school.
✓ Research (Internet or a service like America On-line).
✓ Word processing (papers, letters, e-mail, etc.).
✓ Desktop publishing (newsletters, graphics, etc.).
✓ Design (everything from landscaping to circuit boards).
✓ Using spreadsheets.
✓ Multimedia applications.
✓ Graphics and animation (drafting, drawing, using graphic tools).
✓ Programming and developing new applications for your computer.
✓ Robotics: using computers to control devices.

Typing is a vital skill. Students should be able to type by junior high, meaning thirty words per minute, five or less mistakes, using all fingers on both hands.

Games that teach are great fun and children can learn a great deal. However, the games they are often tempted to spend hours on are pure game entertainment and some aren't very good for them. (See the discussion later in the chapter.)

There are many **programs written to teach.** They're not games, but can replace a text if well written. Unfortunately, many of the programs we've seen are really more like dictionaries with pictures. Computers are not good substitutes for books. Watch out for boring programs of this type.

The computer offers a great and fun way to do **research** through the Internet. Most early web sites weren't really very informative, but that is changing as more and more detailed information can be had on-line. Keep a log of sites visited. (A 3 X 5 index card box works well.)

What do you and your child need to learn on a computer? **Word processing** is a basic skill that's an absolute must for most post-high school institutions. It involves learning a program that allows you to type, correct, stylize, and save your work. A step beyond word processing is desktop publishing.

In its simplest form, **desktop publishing** is taking a written page and making it look professional. For instance, instead of a plain sheet of typewritten words, one could use columns, borders, and art work to make a nice looking newsletter, flyer, resume, or brochure. This kind of application is essential. More and more, people expect to see polished communication from companies with which they do business. For example, would you pay more attention to the business whose flyer has professional looking type, layout and design, or to the business with a crude, hand-lettered flyer? With computer access so widespread, the public's perception of professional and acceptable is at a much higher standard than just five or ten years ago. To compete in the business world or academic environment, computer skills are now a necessity.

Math and business-minded students should begin learning **spreadsheets** and other business programs. Using spreadsheets is something that the science, math, or business student could learn with profit.

Another way children use computers is to **program**, that is, to do something which causes your computer to do something. There are several levels of programming, any of which can be great fun and educational. Some are foundational programming languages and others, like HTML, are written to make programming easy. Sometimes it's hard to tell what is going on with our child and the computer. Many parents think kids are programming when, in fact, they're just making a new game level or format for a favorite game. Hours can be spent doing this to little gain educationally.

Graphics and animation programs are fun for many students and they do have utility. Many people earn a good income creating graphics for others, and kids can learn this, too!

Computer programming is very useful to those students who intend to go into computer engineering, computer science, and even the two year programming courses at the local junior college. Programming languages like Java, C++, and other variations, are good languages to learn. Learning the most important operating systems is also useful: Windows, Mac OS, Unix, and Linux. (2)

Using computers and chips as controllers of devices like robots is good training. Learning functions of various types of chips and putting together ways to use them will be fun for many teens. There's a new 'toy/tool' from MindVision which is used to build computer-controlled Legos™ and Lego™ robots. Clubs and competitions available.

Going On-line: Then there's **communication**. How many people did you know with e-mail addresses five years ago? How many people do you know with them now? An e-mail address is quickly becoming as common as a phone number. It takes a computer and modem to access this important communication tool.

The on-line world is another form of communication that's going to continue to boom in the next few years. The choices can be boggling: do you use a major provider such as America On-line or Prodigy, or direct Internet access through local Internet Service Providers? (ISPs.) You could spend months comparing them, but eventually you'll have to just jump in and actually use one for awhile. Often we don't even know what we will use one for until we hop on board and try it out! Free trial memberships to the major providers can be found bundled with almost any computer magazine or computer. It's a simple process to switch to another server if the one you choose isn't a good fit. (3)

> *Our initial use of on-line servers consisted of visits to homeschool chat rooms by me, Bob's news services, and educational opportunities for our boys. I've since discovered that although I enjoy the chat rooms, I actually don't have the time for them. However, I've done research on the Internet that I never thought I'd do, and I use e-mail far more often than I would have guessed. (I rarely take the time to write letters, but I enjoy zipping off quick notes on the computer - where short and to the point is considered good etiquette! The convenience of no envelope, stamps, or a trip to the mailbox is a plus.)*

> *My oldest son, who NEVER wrote letters, is now an e-mail fan. He's also found areas of interest I would never have known existed. He has taken classes on-line that stretch him intellectually and are easy to attend. He can roll out of bed and sign onto class without me driving him someplace, and there are no bad weather days on-line!*

Warning: Parents should scan the e-mail first. Some people have had the unpleasant experience of receiving nasty letters from miscreants with nothing better to do. Make it a firm rule that adults read the e-mail first so that anything inappropriate can be quickly deleted.

The Big, Bad, Scary Internet: Yes, it's true. There's plenty of bad stuff to be found on the Internet. If you or your child look for it, you can find it. (And sometimes, unfortunately, even when you aren't looking for it.) There are two things to keep in mind. First, on-line time should be monitored at least as closely as TV time. (You are monitoring their TV habits, aren't you?) And many ISPs offer "blocking" services which limit access to inappropriate language for an additional fee. There's also software available which offers parental controls, some of which is available free from web sites. Unfortunately, no blocking system covers everything. Parental supervision is always advised. (3)

Why bother with the Internet? Because it's an incredible gold mine of information. This is where to go for information on any subject you can think of and lots you've never even heard of before. Want to know who died in the Battle of Antietam or who sailed over on the Mayflower? It's there! Need help on a tricky math problem? You can find it! (4)

Your student can take courses via the Internet, too. This may be just the solution for the young high school graduate for whom a college campus is not the answer. We like it because we can provide our children with courses we may not normally teach. See Appendix A.

> *JB attended a course in Logic that met for two hours each week. He listened to a lecture, answered questions via the microphone or keyboard, participated in live, verbal discussions and debates, and didn't even have to put on his shoes! - Maggie (5)*

Software Recommendations: Software changes so rapidly that we can't possibly give you a thorough list of recommended software. Check out the *Home Computer Market*, which is run by the homeschooling Sullivan family. What should you look for in choosing software? Here are some parameters to help you make your selections:
- Programs that require more than yes/no type answers.
- Programs that require problem solving.
- Programs with options for various levels of complexity.
- Programs which simulate real things or processes.
- Programs which inspire them to do more or better work.
- Programs that inform them without talking down to them.

Junior or Senior High School: Already own a computer? Looking for new ways to use it to enhance your child's education? Offer them computer credits for the following:
* Learn business applications which require reading, higher level thinking skills, perseverance, and patience. Great for that bright teen who is ready for a new challenge on the computer.
* HTML - create your own page on the Internet with this language.
* Visual Basic - learn to program in Windows.
* Lotus 1-2-3 or Excel - business spreadsheet programs.
* Quicken or QuickBooks - checkbook programs and business applications.
* Word, Works, etc. for very good word processing programs.
* Corel Draw, PageMaker, Quark - professional desktop publishing

programs.
* AutoCAD - design almost anything, from houses to planes.
* Create and mail newsletters to friends or club members.
* Write penpals around the world (parents should monitor).
* Learn to research topics on the Internet.
* Use the computer as a tool to develop a real or imaginary business.
* Research your family tree.
* Research the college of your dreams and scholarships to get you there.

Elementary Students
* Make signs, letters, posters, charts, graphs, greeting cards, stationery, etc. using various word processing and desktop publishing programs.
* Write and illustrate a book.
* Visit faraway places through Internet connections - find recipes, customs, and other information about a country you're studying.

Pitfalls: Like so many good things, computers have their negative side, too. It's very easy to spend far too much time on the computer. Bright children, particularly those intense, focused sorts, can become so involved in a computer game or application that it's difficult to get them off. It's vital that you establish firm boundaries in the beginning. How much time is allowed for educational software, and how much is allowed for games or fooling around? Set limits and stick to them.

A corollary to this pitfall is spending too much time on it unprofitably. Let's face it, computers didn't exist while we were growing up - at least not as we know them now. Many of us don't know a whole lot about the goings on inside our computers. We use it as we use a car, without paying a lot of attention to the inner works. Then we encounter children who can make the computer sit up and speak, at least as far as we can tell. We can get so impressed with their ability that we seriously overestimate the value of their activity. Even programming shouldn't be allowed to displace math or history. Two hours spent on the computer per day may be too much, especially if it's spent as undirected activity, or devoted to games. **Note:** Children can lose years of educational ground because of too much computer time. However, Joseph Julicher tells us that we should use flexibility because a student might "get on a roll," and stopping could cause him to lose his train of thought. (6)

Children who spend too much time in front of a computer are prone to the same physical effects adults experience, like blurry vision, headaches, stiff necks, etc. Watch for posture problems. Computer desks were not designed for children and the height of the desk, as well as the level of the screen and the placement of the keyboard and mouse are all probably in the wrong place.

Additionally, children can become agitated and disagreeable when their time is up - a sure sign of too much computer time. Watch for this and make decisions based on the age and personality of your child.

Another potential drawback is software. There's real junk out there, folks. You'll find "educational" software that is insipid and entertainment software that's absolutely foul: not just junk, but blasphemous, pornographic, pagan and violent! Pay close attention to what children play at home, and especially to what they're playing at friends' houses. Sit down with them and discuss your absolute standards on what types of games are not appropriate for your family. (Don't be wishy-washy; gifted kids tend to push the limits to the max.)

Some software companies are placing rating systems on their covers. Of course, they may not go far enough for your family - but it's a starting place. Christian magazines are beginning to review software. Here are things to watch out for in the so-called "entertainment" category:

<u>Violence</u> - bad and getting worse in many action games. Detailed, realistic death and destruction.

<u>Language</u> - Many games contain profanity. Beware of the breed of games that are based on movies, and the cartoon games that are anything but childlike.

<u>Sex</u> - lots of sexually explicit games that are intended for adult markets but are sold to kids, also. There are no required ages for buying computer games.

<u>Demon and Devil Games</u> - "Diablo," "Quake," and "Doom," are popular games that should be avoided. Names and covers will give you a pretty good clue as to content. (Watch out for first person role playing games.)

<u>New Age Mysticism</u> - Do you want your child worshiping trees or consulting mystics?

<u>Medieval Role Playing/Fantasy</u> - These can be very seductive, especially for bright, adolescent boys. Does your child really need to spend hours pretending he's a wizard of some sort? (See Galatians 5:19-21.)

Preview games. Use common sense: if a game is contrary to your religion, makes you uncomfortable, or adversely affects your child, don't let it in the house. There are too many worthwhile things to do on the computer than to allow your smart, impressionable child to soak in rot.

Conclusion: The world of computers and the Internet are expanding exponentially, and there are some great opportunities for education available: distance learning, programming and using programs, research, and more. There are also some very real dangers: wasted time, physical problems resulting from computer time, and junk software. Use parental common sense and you will reap benefits from your computer.

Resources & Notes

1) Practical Homeschooling
Absolutely chock-full of useful information! Christian worldview. Mary Pride's bimonthly magazine contains computer software reviews.

Home Life, Inc.
PO Box 1250
Fenton, MO 63026-1850
(800) 346-6322
e-mail: PHSCustSvc@aol.com.
www.home-school.com

Home Computer Market
(800) 827-7420
www.homecomputermarket.com

Founded by the Kihlstadius', now run by the homschooling Sullivan family. Catalog has many hard-to-find award winning titles.

FamilyPC: Secular. Published monthly.

FamilyPC
28 East 28th St.
New York, NY 10016-7930
www.familypc.zdnet.com

2) A good starter for the homeschooled programmer is: *Getting Started in Programming* by Metrowerks. It works for either the PC or the Mac and comes with text, tutorial, CD, and compiler for Pascal, C & C++, Java, and more. Find them at is www.metrowerks.com

3) www.Crosswalk.com offers free web filtering.

America On-line   CompuServ   Prodigy
(800) 827-6364   (800) 848-8199   (800) 776-3449

Looking for a local ISP? Check out the Yellow Pages™ or try one of these web sites:

http://www.boardwatch.com/isp/
http://thelist.iworld.com/

4) A great mega-search engine that searches many other engines at once for you, quickly and easily : http://www.dogpile.com

5) See Escondido Tutorial Service (ETS) in Appendix A.

6) Notes from interview with Joseph Julicher, now a computer engineer, on February 13, 1999.

Question:
What might you like to be when you grow up?

Answers:
Computer programmer or Nintendo employee.
- Mike Stradley, age 13

A marine biologist.
- Laura DiPasquale, age 10

My own boss of a chocolate factory.
- Jessi Smith, age 7

Chapter Thirteen
Apprenticeship is for Gifted Kids, Too

Some of the most expensive programs available to intellectually gifted young people now offer skill components where students actually get to participate hands-on in the subject being studied. They are given the chance to try their hand at what they've been learning. Guess what? With a little creative research, you probably won't have to fork out megabucks to provide your child with such an experience. It may exist right in your own community - for free. It's called apprenticeship!

"Is it my imagination, or is Flossie standing exactly where and how she was last night?" I asked aloud to everyone in general. My 11-year-old daughter Lauren, who is our "farm manager," assured me that it wasn't my imagination and that she had been trying to tell me that Flossie looked sick. We live on two acres out in the country filled with all description of animals, exactly to our middle child's liking. Tending Flossie, our pregnant cow, was but one of her many farm-related duties.

We called the veterinarian who came out and examined Flossie. It was a good thing we called her when we had, because Flossie was in pretty bad shape.

Thus began our relationship with a large animal vet. Being the child who always loved animals, Lauren was extremely interested in all the procedures that this doctor performed on her many visits. One visit prompted the inevitable "Why are your children home during the day?" question and the answer, question, answer, question, answer type conversation that inevitably follows that particular inquiry.

Lauren was so very interested in learning more about how people help sick animals that eventually we asked if she could possibly accompany the doctor on her rounds one day. The answer was positive, and sure enough, the day came when Lauren was invited to go along. She loved it! Then, unexpectedly, she was invited to go along again, and again, and again. Lauren treasured those experiences and longed for more.

As I related this to my homeschooling mentor, Cindy, she suggested that I try to establish a relationship with the vet where Lauren could accompany her once each week in like exchange for volunteering her labor. The labor would be the "dirty work" that needs to be done but no one relishes. The doctor instantly agreed to the arrangement, and the following year was a very happy one for our farm manager. She learned all kinds of things and was performing as a nurse - assistant. Her expertise grew to where she could anticipate what tool was needed next during surgery and was invited to tag along whenever there was something particularly interesting happening.

She even looked forward to going to work on her evening to volunteer. Sometimes she washed the trucks, sometimes she did paper work, sometimes she filled pill bottles, sometimes she cleaned the office. She worked hard and enthusiastically. The arrangement worked out great for everyone involved and was continued into the next year. Our shy middle child became a self-confident, knowledgeable young lady during that time. She also became convinced that whatever she did in her life's work, it would include animals and the outdoors.

The following year it became apparent to the veterinarian and her secretary that the business had grown to the point where they needed to hire some part-time help. Who do you suppose they offered the position to? Of course, Lauren was exceedingly pleased. It was not only her first paying job, it was a job she was skilled at and loved. - Janice

Sarah worked in or out of veterinarians' offices the entire time she was in high school. She cleaned stalls or cages, took vital signs, assisted in surgery, learned to read x-rays, and more. It was a great set of experiences. It is also required for admission into vet school according to the three places she has interviewed (Texas A&M, Ohio State University and Cornell). And like Janice's teen, Sarah ended up receiving good wages for the experience. Oh, yes, Sarah started nearly every job (being a military family, we moved frequently) by volunteering to do odd jobs, cleaning stalls and cages. She worked hard on even the most menial work (those cages were clean!) and was eventually offered paying jobs. She would spend her lunch hours reading the vet manuals and asking questions. This behavior could not go unnoticed and this winter she called the veterinarian's office she worked for two summers ago, and was given an immediate position. Many vets say that for insurance reasons they cannot hire underage people, but volunteers can do a lot of helping around a vet's office or stable which does not interfere with insurance (no animal contact). Sooner or later, the job opening will come. Once, Sarah was actually turned down but volunteered to work until I arrived to pick her up. She did get the job. Be persistent and helpful. - Kathleen

Apprenticeship, internship, mentorship. No matter by what name it's called; it's a good idea. Through apprenticeship, children have the chance to put skills to work and learn how to interact with adults in situations similar to the ones they will likely face upon graduation from their home education or conventional school program.

A friend of ours related this experience about her son:

BJ was kind of a quiet kid - like his dad. He enjoyed playing the piano and messing around with his friends. But one thing really got him excited: computers. As soon as he finished his studies each day, he would spend whatever time he could on the computer. His mom got him books on programming, and he pored over them. What he read, he put into action on their Mac. Over the years, his interest grew. He really wasn't sure he was interested in going to college; he was really sure he was interested in computers. After careful consideration, his parents took the money they had saved for his college education and bought him a state-of-the-art computer, printer and many peripherals. He had learned so much about computers and programming over the years, they believed he would learn what he needed to know to be a valuable employee or entrepreneur if just given time and exposure to the equipment. Right about then, BJ began volunteering in the TV studio at their church. He started out sweeping the floors and emptying the waste cans. Folks began to notice that he had an incredible amount of interest and aptitude concerning the use of computers in television and movie production. BJ was even able to help them through various difficulties. Soon a paying position opened up; BJ applied for the job and got it. Then this homeschool graduate began making good money doing what he loved. Now, years later, his reputation in his city for being the one to call when it comes to problems that arise in computers and film production is well established.

Experience is the best teacher, or so the saying goes. Many young people are taking advantage of the enormous opportunities available to them as home educated students. The flexible schedules they usually possess, and the ability to take the time to really focus on an area of interest are very valuable and envied by many of their traditionally-schooled peers.

Children may work in several different capacities before they find something that excites them and holds their interest. Previously, Lauren (being the descendant of a long lineage of country folk!) volunteered for a couple of years as an interpreter at the agricultural museum her grandmother helped found; BJ worked as a horticulturist in a large greenhouse. These were valuable learning experiences for both of them and helped them to go on to self-confidently try other things. Real life experiences in the real workday world are tremendous teachers. Additionally, with proper record-keeping, high school credits may be awarded for work done while an apprentice. For a detailed look at apprenticeship, see Inge Cannon's *Mentoring Your Teen* (1).

But, these opportunities usually don't knock on your door. It takes an alert, caring adult to search out the possibilities, turn occurrences into opportunities, and encourage their child to actively participate. Even an outgoing child can be timid about new social situations. In other words you have to ask for a job or a volunteer position. Sometimes it is easier to start by joining an organization of volunteers. The Red Cross is just one example of this type of organization.

> *Joseph was a Red Cross volunteer at thirteen. They put him to work on their computer system, getting it organized and set up (back in the days of Apples and Ataris). He did a good job and got a good recommendation. That helped him get a job when he was sixteen at the local computer store where he sold computers and eventually did network setups for businesses in St. Louis, MO. Later, during college, he landed a job programming for Children's Services in Dayton, OH. All of these opportunities began with a home computer and a volunteer job with the Red Cross - Kathleen*

You may have questions about possible opportunities and whether they fit with your child's personality. Use the informative test from Career Direct for some guidance in this area. (2) What are your child's interests? Are there opportunities in your community where they could garner some hands-on experience in those areas of interest? It wasn't easy for me to approach the veterinarian on Lauren's behalf. I was timid about the whole idea. But, after all, what more could she do than say "No"? As is so often the case, she didn't. There are many adults who would be pleased to share their vocation with an interested young person.

> *JB volunteered one day each week at the local Christian bookstore. Two years earlier, he was volunteering at the public library. Hmmmm. Are books in his future? I wonder... Maggie*

Resources & Notes

1) Cannon, Inge and Ronald (1993). *Mentoring Your Teen.*
   Education +Plus
   PO Box 1350
   Taylors, SC 29687
   (864) 609-5411
   www.edplus.com

2) Career Direct

   Crown Financial Ministries
   PO Box 1476
   Gainesville, GA 30503-1476
   (770) 534-1000
   www.cfcministry.org

Question:
What are some of the difficulties/frustrations you have experienced with your child's schooling?

Answers:
"Trying to find things that are a challenge to her is a challenge to me."

"Lack of motivation for book work."

"I feel unable to challenge them."

"My child is only motivated by what fascinates her. She's bored with regular studies - even when we need them to lay a foundation for her interests. She's a loner - never gets along with others - doesn't know how to be with people."

Chapter Fourteen
Preparing for High School and College

What is the "ideal" high school experience? There are many "ideals" in planning for high school, just as there are for most facets of our lives. With high school, as with the rest of your homeschooling, do your very best and don't get caught up in a feeling of inadequacy just because Mrs. B is teaching her three teens Latin, physics, and trigonometry! Everyone has strengths and weaknesses just as every family has interests and special hobbies or abilities. No homeschooling family will look like another, nor should they. If one year is less than banner, strive for improvement the next. Love your teens and give them as many opportunities to learn as you can. Help them to learn study skills, life skills, and give them opportunities to stretch and grow (and sometimes fail!) Help them to see the practical applications of your faith so that they will want to emulate you. Whether or not your student has chemistry lab or AP level courses is not nearly as important as having a personal relationship with their Lord.

Having said that, this chapter provides some "ideals" in preparing for and completing high school at home.

With most students, it's best to assume they will be attending college and plan their course work that way. This keeps their options open. Begin by researching your state's and/or homeschool association's requirements for high school. Additionally, consider buying the *Guide to PA Homeschoolers Diploma* by Howard and Susan Richman. (1) This excellent booklet has many examples of ways to earn high school credits and prepare for college. PA homeschoolers may receive credit if they do any **one** of the following:

- Over two-thirds of textbook
- 120 daily logged entries
- 120 hours of logged study
- 10 page research paper
- College course
- Passed AP Exam

What requirements (if any) do you have in your state? Your state may not have requirements for graduation, but there may be requirements for entry into a state supported college. Check with your state homeschool organization. For more information, try HSLDA. (2)

Making a Plan for High School

Take advantage of homeschooling and start planning in sixth grade!

❶Make a list of all required courses. You may have several kinds of requirements to meet:
> ⇨ Courses required by the college. (3)
> ⇨ Courses required by the state. (4)
> ⇨ Course required by a homeschool association. (2)
> ⇨ Courses required by the parents. (5)
> ⇨ Courses determined by the student's interests.

❷Use the high school course planner in Appendix D to spread out the courses over six years (or four years if your teen is already in high school).

❸ Then, with your student, discuss options for electives. Keep your student's interests and abilities in mind as you plan. Electives don't have to be planned all at once. Be flexible and allow your student room for changing interests and maturity.

For college-bound students, minimum requirements may not be enough. For example, perhaps your student isn't required to study a foreign language and doesn't particularly want to, but the liberal arts college he's considering requires two years of a foreign language. This could lead to problems in admission if you do not find out these requirements for that college early enough to take the courses. Don't wait until the senior year to find this out!

Many colleges require three years of math, but don't specify what math one must take. If possible, choose the standard "college-prep" math sequence of Algebra 1 and 2 and geometry. A student interested in math or science would do well to consider more math; like calculus or trigonometry. Many students are ready for Algebra 1 in the eighth grade. Take it early and have more time for upper level math.

There are several reasons for researching colleges early, at least by eleventh grade, if not tenth:

❏ By having some idea of which colleges your student might attend, you can better choose appropriate high school classes.

❏ The extra time will allow you to more thoroughly research scholarship and financial aid options.

❐ The extra time will allow your student to visit or correspond with the schools, ask more questions, and then do a great job on the applications.

"They know enough who know who to learn."

- Henry Adams

❐ Your student will have more time to prepare for, and more opportunities to take the SAT or ACT for colleges which require certain scores.

Using High School to Prepare for College

① Read the stories of other homeschoolers and how they got into the college of their choices.

② Make an academic plan covering 6 (or 4) years. Do this in sixth or seventh grade. It's easy for gifted students to begin high school in the seventh grade year. See Resources and Notes for information on books about homeschoolers and college.(6)

③ Do take some Advanced Placement courses. (7) You don't have to take the tests, but taking the courses will prepare for college courses and weighs heavily on college admissions. Great challenge for gifted kids! Many homeschoolers take the exams and score well enough to receive college credit.

④ Add electives, keeping college requirements and student interests in mind.

⑤ Keep excellent records; a portfolio or file.

⑥ Keep a professional looking transcript for all course work and extracurricular activities.

⑦ Prepare for and take PSAT, SAT, SAT II, or ACT, and AP tests as required. PA Homeschoolers offer on-line AP courses. (1) Give your student 1/4 credit for Test Prep, Preparing for the PSAT or whatever set of tests he/ she will be taking. Our children took the SAT several times, improving their test taking skills each time.

⑧ Begin to research colleges in the sophomore year, or junior year at the latest. By the eleventh grade, you should have a list of five or six colleges you're interested in and already have received their materials. This is important!!

⑨ Optional: yearly grade report. Some parents may wish to send it to colleges, so it should be as professional looking as possible.

I did not send in grades in this form. The only grades colleges saw of my students were the ones on the transcript. I did use a grade card for a permanent record from which I took their grades for the transcript. This saved the trouble it would have been to look up all those grades since, they were all on one card, even the grades given by the music teacher. - Kathleen

⑩ Pay attention to the deadlines for colleges! This is very important!

College Admissions

There are those who may tell you that your homeschooled high school student will never get into a good college. **Listen carefully:** That is simply not true! Homeschoolers have been accepted and have excelled in colleges across the nation, including Ivy League schools! Homeschoolers are even being recruited by colleges who have seen how well these independent, well-educated, young people do on college campuses. We've seen advertisements from some Christian colleges offering scholarships to homeschoolers in order to attract home educated youths to their campus. Perhaps most importantly, we've seen the proof in our friends' and our own children's admissions to various colleges, universities, and even Military Academies. You **can** provide your student with a quality education, tailor made for his gifts and abilities.

College is much easier to get into today than it was years ago. Even if a student can't get into the school of their first choice, they will most likely be able to get into an acceptable school. However, scholarships are very competitive. Important points to consider concerning admissions:

CHOOSE YOUR COLLEGE CAREFULLY
Certainly your student should have input, but remember, you are turning your son or daughter over to this institution for the next four years, so be sure it's the right place for them. Begin research by the tenth grade, if at all possible. Write for catalogs. Check out Lovejoy's or Peterson's from your local library. "Visit" campuses by checking out their home pages on the Internet. Call or write for brochures and even videos of colleges that interest you. Ask people you like and respect what college they recommend. Ask, ask, ask!

Looking for a Christian college? Many are "Christian" in name or tradition only. Where do you stand in your beliefs, and how closely do you require the school to match them? What are their rules and regulations? Too strict? Too lenient? Ask tough questions. Go beyond those glossy brochures and sales pitches.

Are you looking for a secular school with a certain major and lots to offer? Some secular schools are fairly mainstream, and others are hothouses of radical indoctrination. We've heard stories of parents horrified to find out after their child has moved in that their dorms are co-ed or that the student is assigned to room with a homosexual. Carefully read the literature, especially the student handbook and campus policies. Does this school have lots of strong organizations where your student can find support and fellowship? Ask many questions. There's more at stake than just academics; choose wisely.

NARROW IT DOWN

At some point you and your student will need to narrow down the list. It isn't really practical to do an in-depth study of more than six or so schools. Find out their specific prerequisites: course work and test scores, and application deadlines. When you have a handful of schools you're truly interested in, it's time to call. The sophomore or junior years are good times for this activity, but wait no later.

Because scholarships are competitive, if your gifted student has distinguished himself in any number of ways, now is the time to blow his horn. **Here are just a few examples of how gifted homeschooled students may stand out:**

- ❖ Scored 1400 on the PSAT or SAT.
- ❖ Scored 1200 on the PSAT or SAT at a much younger age than normal.
- ❖ 4.0 average (measurable) with fairly high achievement test scores.
- ❖ Started and operated a home business.
- ❖ Finished high school in less than the standard four years.
- ❖ Musical, athletic, artistic, in measurable ways.
- ❖ Gifted leader: president of this and that. Started this, runs that.
- ❖ Organized volunteer work teams, etc.
- ❖ Outstanding in terms of community service.

Objectively evaluate your student and focus on how they shine!
Obviously, there are many more examples of outstanding students. Write down their achievements and have them in front of you when calling the Admissions Officer and say, "I have a gifted student who's interested in attending your school. Here's what she's accomplished: _____. We're looking for scholarships. What do you have to offer?"

Now you should be able to narrow down the colleges to just a few. If you still don't know which college is right, if at all possible visit the campuses. The environment is important. There's nothing like actually talking to students and sitting in on a class to help decide if this is the right school or not.

TESTS - TAKE THE TIME TO PREPARE; IT WILL PAY OFF!

Prepare for the tests diligently and test frequently. Once a year is good. The junior year tests will probably be the results the colleges will see because senior year tests must be completed in the fall in order to get the results in time for the admissions deadlines. There are a few local schools which have rolling admissions or a low number of applicants, but it is best to plan to take the tests early.

Following is a list of widely used exams for college acceptance and credit. Many homeschoolers have been successful in taking and passing them. Send for the information, read, and follow the directions carefully. There are books available to help prepare for each and every possible examination. If you can't find them at your library or bookstore, then certainly from:

College Board Publishing
2 College Way
PO Box 1100
Forrester Center, WV 25438
(800) 323-7155
www.collegeboard.org

**PSAT/NMSQT - Preliminary Scholastic Assessment Test /
National Merit Scholarship Qualifying Test**This test measures verbal reasoning, mathematical reasoning, and writing abilities. It's traditionally the practice test for the SAT, as it contains the same kinds of questions and estimates your potential SAT score. Eligible juniors who take the PSAT/NMSQT in October will automatically be entered into the Merit Program (or sophomores who plan to skip the last year of high school). Merit Scholarship Awards will be given to about 7,000-8,000 students based on their scores. Preregistration and a fee are required. Sign up for the PSAT in early September at the high school counselor's office. This test is taken in the school during school hours. When you register and pay your fee, a counselor should give you a practice book. For more information:

PSAT/NMSQT
PO Box 6720
Princeton, NJ 08541-6720
(609) 771-7070   (609) 882-4118 TTY

SAT - Scholastic Aptitude Test
SAT 1 (formerly SAT)

The SAT 1 is a three hour test, primarily consisting of multiple choice questions that measure verbal, mathematical, and writing abilities. SAT 1 is administered six times per year. Preregistration and a fee are required. The test is administered in a local high school on Saturdays. A student must register with the College Board and will receive a ticket to get into the testing. For a registration packet and a free copy of *Taking the SAT 1*, contact a local high school or write:

College Board SAT Program
PO Box 6200
Princeton, NJ 08541-6200

AP - Advanced Placement

Advanced Placement Program, offered by the College Board, gives high school students the opportunity to receive college credit for what they've learned in high school or on their own. (1) Tests are given only in May by participating high schools. Students must register for the tests before April. For free brochures on this program write:

Advanced Placement Program
PO Box 6670
Princeton, NJ 08541-6670

For names of a school near you which administer the exams, write:
AP Services
PO Box 6671
Princeton, NJ 08541-6671

CLEP - College Level Examination Program

The College Level Examination Program offers credit-by-examination in a wide range of subjects commonly required for college undergraduates. Taking and passing these tests can save you a lot of time and money! These tests are administered at colleges across the country. We've found them to be a wonderful source of inexpensive college credits. Write for your free CLEP Colleges booklet:

CLEP
PO Box 6601
Princeton, NJ 08541-6601

Resources & Notes

1) *Guide to PA Homeschoolers Diploma.* On-line classes and more.
Pennsylvania Homeschoolers
RR 2 Box 117
Kittanning, PA 16201
www.pahomeschoolers.com

2) Home School Legal Defense Association (HSLDA)
PO Box 3000
Purcellville, VA 20134
(540) 338-5600
www.hslda.org

3) Write prospective colleges for viewbooks and student handbooks.

4) Consult a local homeschool support network for this information.

5) This is your own list. Many parents require certain courses like preparing for marriage, home finances, home and car repair, etc.

6) Cohen, Cafi (1997). *And What About College?, Homeschooling: The Teen Years,* and *Homeschooler(s) College Admissions Handbook*
375 Plancha Way
Arroyo Grande, CA 93420
Cafi@worldnet.att.net
www.homeschoolteenscollege.net
(Very useful site.)

Shelton , Barbara (1993). *Senior High: A Home-Designed Form-U-La*
Howshall Home Publications
PO Box 1750
Eatonville, WA 98328-1750
(360) 832-8845
BEShelton@aol.com

Schofield, Mary. *High School Handbook: Junior and Senior High School at Home.*
widely available from Amazon, etc.

Julicher, Kathleen and Mark, (1992). *Survival Tools For Homeschooling Teens*. A seminar: 6 hours. Tapes with book - $35.00
Castle Heights Press, Inc.

7) See Note 1) for more AP prep information.

Chapter Fifteen
Record Keeping

Keeping track of any child's progress is important, but it becomes especially meaningful for a gifted child, for several reasons. First, it is quite probable you will pursue many different avenues of education for your child. Because you may not use textbooks, your homeschool may not look like a traditional school. In order to help you document your schooling for future educational goals, and in order to satisfy any legal requirements in your state, it is important to keep accurate records. Gifted children are also quite likely to attend some form of a higher education, and good records may be needed in order to place them in an appropriate program or college.

Lastly, record keeping is important because you will never be able to remember it all. It's like that first year of babyhood; if you don't write it down, you'll probably forget it. It's always a blessing to go back through baby books and journals, remembering. Good records of your child's education will accomplish the same thing. Imagine forgetting to put on that application that Johnny won a major award. It seems hard to believe, but it's very possible to forget in the heat of filling out all those forms. **Keep good records. You'll never regret it.**

Your portfolio, or personal file, isn't intended for college. A certain college may want you to provide one (especially private, liberal arts schools), but generally speaking you'll use the information in your files simply to fill out college (or scholarship) applications. We once heard of a mom who literally sent in an entire box of information, including all of the papers her child had completed through the years. It's hard to believe anyone ever looked at them. Even small colleges can have thousands applying, and it's unrealistic to expect them to go through that volume of material. Keeping a few representative papers of major courses and final exams can't hurt, but don't send it to a college unless they ask for more data, or unless it's very unusual material, like a published poem or a book.

If you're following a standard textbook approach, it's simple to develop a notebook or portfolio of your student's papers, tests, etc. Group papers by subject, and within the subject, group them chronologically. Store them neatly in a three-ring binder. Keep a grade sheet. By tracking this information you'll have records which are easier to go through when the time for applications arrives.

If you're using a unit study approach, we highly recommend *The Home Education CopyBook & Planning Guide* for the forms you may want to use

If you're using a unit study approach, we highly recommend *The Home Education CopyBook & Planning Guide* for the forms you may want to use to document and organize this creative approach to schooling. (1)

If you use an eclectic approach, your notebook can hold a combination of items that show regular and thorough schooling has taken place. See Appendix D for various forms helpful for record keeping.

RECORDS:

❑ A year-end report card

A year end report card is a standard document. You may choose to use letter grades, number grades, pass/fail, or no grades at all, depending on your state's requirements. Many people prefer to write a short evaluation under each subject, citing the student's strengths, accomplishments, and weaknesses. Be as concise and objective as possible.

Be aware, however, that traditional institutions of higher learning are most familiar with letter grades. You may be creating a problem if you don't use them with your high school student. It's best to make it as easy as possible for an Admissions Officer to understand where your student is academically. Letter grades are the most widely used vehicle for conveying this information, especially in high school transcripts.

❑ Book list

One document that may prove to be quite valuable later is a book list. This list should show a large, representative sample of books your child has read. You may prefer to list them chronologically, although it may be more helpful to list them by subject matter. One friend of ours pointed out that when she enrolled her gifted son in public school after homeschooling, the school elected to skip him two grades, right into high school. They said the depth and variety of books he had chosen to read helped indicate his maturity and educational level.

❑ Awards

Parents sometimes ask about how far to go back when referring to awards. We suggest that if the project is high school level, include it. If the award is for something very distinctive, like the National Latin Exam Summa Cum Laude Award, even if your child was younger, include it.

❑ Clubs and offices held

Include any professional organizations your child has joined, especially those which are usually considered to be for adults. An example is the Dayton Amateur Radio Association, which two of our children joined and worked with on several events.

❏ <u>Job descriptions</u> (paid/unpaid, short/ long term)
Don't forget to record the names, addresses, and phone numbers of people who supervised your child. You will probably need these later on for recommendations or forms.

❏ <u>Project descriptions</u>
Be sure to include results of projects. For example, if your child worked with Habitat for Humanity, record how many houses he helped to build and any thank you notes, etc. If for a job, did she save the business money or time? Record it. Be sure to have photos of their work to include in a portfolio-type application.

❏ <u>Community service projects</u>
See "Project descriptions."

❏ <u>Hobbies</u>
Many hobbies provide the basis for a career and so are important to the education of a homeschooler. They may be interconnected to other items in this list, like jobs, awards, and projects. That's fine; just keep them recorded for future use.

❏ <u>Course work outside the home</u>
      A. Tutors.
      B. On-line courses.
      C. College courses (transcripts, address, phone, etc.).
      D. Correspondence courses (transcripts are needed here, too).

❏ <u>Letters of recommendation</u>
Obtain these from job supervisors, or mentors, or teachers.
Important: Get letters written when an event or job is done, not three years later. Don't send originals to a college or scholarship office.

❏ <u>Portfolio notebooks</u>
These are well worth doing, but add to them on a monthly or semester basis. Doing an entire year's worth at one time can be quite daunting! Consider a portfolio an important school record, as well as a wonderful memory book your child will always cherish.

❏ <u>Transcripts</u>
Developing a transcript is easy. Use a computer to generate a good looking transcript. While you're at it, create a diploma, invitations to the graduation, and thank you notes.

UNIVERSITIES EXPECT CERTAIN DATA FROM TRANSCRIPTS:

❐ Name, address, phone number, gender, birth date, and Social Security number of the student (usually optional).

❐ Name of the school, address, phone number (if different from the student's, as in a satellite school situation).

❐ Date of graduation. This would be the date of actual graduation you've decided it to be, not the projected date of graduation.

❐ List of all courses taken for credit and the number of credit hours earned. Be sure to order transcript copies from those institutions; and ask that they be sent directly to the next school. Universities will want an original. Keep a copy for your own records.

❐ Total number of credits earned for high school. If you have college hours too, you may wish to count them for high school credit. However, some colleges may not accept them as college courses if you've counted them towards high school graduation, even if they were actually college level courses. Check it out.

❐ Grades are optional. If you include grades, be sure to include the grading scale.

❐ Optional: Years in which the student earned the credit for courses. We recommend you leave this out. An example is: Your child took Latin I in seventh grade, but it was actually high school level. You would note that on the transcript without detailing the year in which it was taken. It helps to use a "by subject" method of organization instead of a "by year" method.

❐ Be sure to include the level of computer literacy if your child can use a computer. Some colleges require this course and its record on the transcript.

❐ Include all those extra credits earned with projects, independent study, and internships. Carnegie Credits: 1 credit = 150 actual hours, one-half credit = 75 hours, 1/4 credit = 35-40 hours. (There is some leeway in the amount of actual hours, ranging from ~ 120 - 150 hours per credit.)

❐ Test results from: SAT I, SAT II, ACT, PSAT, or other achievement tests at the high school level.

❐ Include the National Merit Scholarship Qualifying selection index and rank if it has been decided already, and if the student did well. (2)

❐ If you have earlier high scores from Talent Search, for example, include them, but be sure to add the grade or age of the student at the time of testing. Don't assume they will read the score report that closely.

❐ Add an educational history section if your student has an unusual one. For instance, if while in a regular school in the ninth grade he was accepted into an IB (International Baccalaureate) program, or went to Ireland with Johns Hopkins CTY, include that information. We encourage you to note whether your child even qualified for a course.

A transcript is a profile of your student and their education.
Make it as complete and as accurate as possible. This isn't the time to be modest! Leaving anything notable out is just as dishonorable as inserting an untruth. If it happened, record it. In the presentation you actually give to the university (transcripts and paperwork), you may decide to leave out the years in which your child took classes and grades for the subjects he studied. Leaving off the grades encourages the school to look at the subjects your child has studied, rather than merely his grade point average (GPA).

Resources & Notes

1) Von Duyke, Kathy (199_). *The Home Education CopyBook & Planning Guide.* This book is a treasure trove of reproducible forms. Included are planning forms, working forms, portfolio forms, record keeping forms, posted forms, plus make and do forms that can be personalized and used year after year.

Kathy von Duyke
429 Lewisville Road
P.O. Box 274
New London, PA 19360

2) PSAT/NMSQT

P.O. Box 6720
Princeton, NJ 08541-6720
(609) 771-7070; (609) 882-4118 TTY
www.collegeboard.com

Question:
What gets your child(ren) excited?

Answers:
Debate
Building things - cardboard and lots of tape are his biggest joy
Legos
Geography
Animals
Almost anything!
Challenges, contests
Experiments
Anything hands-on
Beauty
Out-of-doors
Computers
Gadgets
Projects
Making contributions to society
Field trips
Feeling personally connected to what she's learning about
Drama
Reading!
Making money

Chapter Sixteen
Mentors For Parents

Wouldn't it be great to know someone who has walked the path you're on already; one who has an abundance of great advice for educating your gifted child? It's nothing less than a blessing when we find such a person. They can share the results of their experiences, both good and bad. Resources can be passed on, as can methods and practical tips.

You can be such a person! There's someone out there who knows less than you about giftedness; someone who could greatly benefit from your knowledge. Make the effort to reach out and offer to lend an ear when needed.

At the same time, look for someone from whom you can learn. Each of us benefits from the counsel of wise friends and, in turn, can be a blessing to someone else along the way. By both being a mentor and looking to a mentor, you'll grow in your skills and abilities as a teacher, as a parent, and as a human being.

You may want to consider starting a support group for parents of gifted. Even if there's just a small homeschooling population in your area, you'll very likely find a few gifted children within it. Ask around. Check with your state or local homeschool organization. Look for gifted information at conferences. Place a notice in a support group newsletter. Start a gifted newsletter with tips and advice applicable to your area. (1)

Ask for gifted workshops at your state conventions. State leaders are always trying to meet the needs of homeschooling parents. Some are already offering workshops, others probably would if the need were made known to them.

A mentoring relationship can go beyond one-on-one, to organizations, idea exchanges, and projects like this book - which is our way of mentoring as many people as possible.

The benefits are well worth pursuing. If you're feeling isolated, if you consider giftedness a real "problem," are longing for someone to talk to who understands, or just want to find the best possible opportunities for your student, reaching out is the way to go.

I remember feeling overwhelmed at times, wondering how my husband and I would be able to provide our boys with the type of education we wanted for them. Where would we find what we needed to know about useful materials, high school credits, AP courses, SAT's, scholarships, and more? God blessed me with a new friend. Janice has a highly gifted son four years older than our oldest. She's graciously answered my questions and has been a constant source of encouragement. Learning from her family's experiences, we've made better decisions for our sons. It isn't always easy to reach out, and it may not always work, but when it does it's well worth the effort. - Maggie

Resources & Notes

1) Hall, Kathy (1998) in Indianapolis, Indiana heads up a homeschool support group for families with gifted children. She also is the author of a classical curriculum, *Hall's Curriculum Guide for the Classical Homeschool K-8th grades*.

> Kathy Hall
> 7904 Dawson Drive
> Fishers, IN 46038

Lita Oates is the editor of a newsletter, *Families Learning at Home*, which is available on the Internet for $10.00 per year. She homeschools a gifted student and has a master's degree in gifted education.
Subscribe to at: LrningAtHm@aol.com

> Janice Baker
> 526 Blackiston Road
> Clayton, DE 19938
> cbaker37@netscape.net

> Maggie Hogan
> PO Box 2333
> Cheswold, DE 19936
> (877) 492-8081
> Maggie@BrightIdeasPress.com

> Kathleen Julicher
> 106 Caldwell Drive
> Baytown, TX 77520
> Julicher@aol.com

Chapter Seventeen
Looking Back - Seth's Perspective

My name is Seth Baker. Let me start off by saying that I don't really think of myself as being "gifted." More like "quick minded." I seem to grasp concepts a little more clearly and quickly than most of the people I come into contact with, but I'm not really a genius or anything like that. I think this is an important distinction to make at the outset because the fact is that if my mom hadn't pulled me out of school and let me work at my own pace, I would not have gotten as far as I have today. If I had been in a public (or private for that matter) school, I would probably have gotten good grades, but as far as academic achievement goes, I wouldn't have any real advantage. The point of all this is to say that a lot of times, it takes special attention and interest in a particular student for that student to cultivate what may be a natural ability to succeed.

I should start by giving you a brief history of me. Before I started going to school, my mom taught me through preschool and kindergarten. This really did a couple of things. One, it gave me a good start and confidence that I could achieve what I wanted to. Two, it was the beginning of a good relationship between my mom and me. We really just had a lot of fun while I learned to write (first my name then more complex things like 'cat') and the basics of reading. I started first grade at a Christian school just before my sixth birthday. I think I liked it a lot (my memory is a little foggy on this point). While in the second grade, my family moved in the middle of the year, and I had to switch schools. During the time we were between schools, again Mom kept me caught up with my work. I stayed at the new school for all of third grade and fourth grade. I was getting perfect marks on my report card and I was starting to get bored out of my skull.

So, when I started fifth grade, it was at home with Mom. I absolutely loved it. At first, it was just great fun to get to tell my friends I didn't go to school anymore and that I was done with my work by noon. But what I liked best was that if I already understood a subject area, we didn't have to spend another couple of weeks going over and over and over it. It was at this point that I realized that I had spent most of the fourth grade reviewing the third grade. It upset me that so much time had been wasted. (It wasn't until much later that I realized that even most of high school is spent reviewing previous material.)

We had a great time through the sixth grade. Then I started to get bored again. I convinced Mom that I already knew virtually all the material in the seventh grade textbooks, and she got me eighth grade books. I really think that this was the turning point in my schooling career. At the same time that we realized I was getting pretty good at this "student" thing, we realized that we didn't actually have to follow any kind of traditional grade system. So I skipped seventh grade altogether. I was ecstatic.

In much the same fashion, as we continued the high school experience, I skipped the ninth and eleventh grades. Like I said before, I don't think this was because I was "smart" or "gifted," I just caught on to this stuff and didn't have to go over it time and time again. I have a sneaking suspicion that a whole lot of kids in the world could breeze through school a lot faster (and with far fewer headaches) if they were just given the chance. Another important thing happened at this time. When I was 12-years-old I took one class at the University of Delaware. It was an introductory math course. This was the most challenged I had ever found myself as a student. So, of course, I loved it (plus I got to tell everyone I was in college). I guess I really didn't care for the course work itself - I hated math and it included a lot of homework - but just knowing that I was moving at my own pace made it worthwhile. When the grades came out and I got an A, I remember thinking, "What's the big deal with college?" But it was great.

The next semester, I took pre-calculus. This introduced another first in my life. The teacher, after each test, would tell us what percent of the class got an A, a B, etc. She would also put the highest score on the test on the blackboard for us to aspire to. It didn't take me long to realize that most of the time, the high score on the board corresponded with the score on my test. When I realized this, it evoked two emotions in me. One, it made me laugh. I thought it was great fun showing up a bunch of college students five years older than I. Second, it kind of disappointed me. It was disappointing to think that college students coming out of our highly acclaimed educational system couldn't do better than some 13-year-old who just did his homework and his best.

After another year of taking math courses at the University, I had also accumulated enough credits to meet the requirements for graduation from high school. So, when I was fourteen, I graduated from high school. I applied to Delaware State University (closer to home than the U of D), and rather surprisingly - to me at least - they accepted me for full time study. [Authors' note - with a full scholarship.] I graduated summa cum laude with my B.S. in Business Administration when I was eighteen.

Looking back now, there really isn't much I would want to change about the way I did things. Sometimes I get to thinking that it would have been nice to be involved more with my peer group. I really didn't have many friends growing up. My favorite theory about this is that people my age just didn't understand me. I must have seemed like some kind of freak. Kids have a natural tendency to dislike what they don't understand. Actually, adults often exhibit the same tendency. Another possible reason is that I was a very distant person. My sister says I was such a nerd that no one wanted to be near me. (I am not, and have never been, a nerd!) Maybe it was just because I never really made much effort to make friends. I'm at a point in my life now where I do make just such an effort (and in fact I do have friends these days), but a few years ago I was never really that interested. Come to think of it, I guess I just didn't like people my age very much. I certainly never felt a need to be accepted by my peers.

So, what's the point of this whole discussion? Well, any kid who is truly gifted, or who moves through the educational system at an advanced pace, needs to realize that they may have difficulty (for whatever reason) making as many friends as the people around them have. This is a relevant point to raise. The whole socialization question is often raised as an objection to homeschooling as an institution. It's even more of an issue for gifted kids. Thinking about it, maybe it was to my advantage to be relatively alone. I was never caught up in any of the distracting little things that take away from kids' study time. But it may have been advantageous to practice social skills a fair amount more than I did.

Another point is that when I started at Delaware State University when I was fourteen, I never really felt out of place. Even though Delaware State is an historically black land grant school (and I'm quite white) and everyone there was eighteen (and I was four years younger) it never occurred to me to feel like I didn't belong there. Maybe just because I was so used to doing things people my age never did, I was numb to feeling awkward. Whatever the case, it never bothered me to be where I was. I've always trusted God to lead me where I need to go, and then there I'll be.

Finally, let me say that you ultimately get out of life what you put into it. I don't think it's possible to overstress the importance of setting goals for yourself. From my own experience, I've discovered that my mind-set going into something greatly effects the outcome of the situation. There have been semesters where my goal was just to get through with minimum effort, and there have been semesters when I knew that nothing short of straight "A's" would satisfy me. And you can guess when I had the better performance. It has been a lot of work to get to where I am. At the outset, most of the tough and tedious work was done by Mom. Lately, it has been a lot of work for me. But throughout my experience, year after year, a lot of dedication and concentration have been required. Whether it was arguing with administrators as to why a 12-year-old kid should be allowed into a college course, or the grueling daily dosage of course work, someone has been very busy right along.

In the end, (or at least from where I am now) it's been worth it. I'm happy to have graduated from college. It makes me feel good, and no doubt it makes my parents feel good, too. We always say "as you sow, so shall you reap" and it couldn't be more true. Every reward in life, by necessity, has to be the result of some action. Choose each action wisely.

[Authors' Note: Since this was written, Seth was accepted into University of Delaware's MBA program and graduated at age twenty-one.]

THE GIFTED CHILD AND CONTESTS

Entering contests can be great motivation for the gifted child. After all, the word "contests" brings to mind "challenges", "rewards", "skills" and "abilities"... Contests provide a good, constructive use of the child's time, thus alleviating boredom. Spending an afternoon creating Lego models (see contest listings) is a good example of a boredom buster.

They can explore new ideas and develop their creative energies while working on various projects for the contest(s). Your gifted child may be more willing to move out of his comfort zone and try a new skill or activity if he has the incentive inherent in contests. Also, certain ones can be used as an extension of something your child is studying in school; for instance, the "DuPont Challenge Science Essay Awards" or "Pizza Hut's Book It! Program."

...And, of course, there is always the motivation of a possible prize! Pins, ribbons, cash, t-shirts and more, "sweeten-the pot". Who doesn't enjoy an award for their hard work?!

Following is a listing of contests you may want to consider. There are many other contests available. Keep an eye out for local contests in your area. We know students who have entered coloring, writing, photography and essay contests (to name a few) that are sponsored by the library, local businesses, newspapers and organizations in our area. Prizes have ranged from certificates to t-shirts to scholarship money!

One more idea...why don't you and/or your child design a contest and promote it in your homeschool group, church, or town? Our homeschool group has held poetry, essay and art contests where each entrant submitted $1.00 to help offset costs. The winners received gift certificates to local bookstores and for art supplies. Use your imagination! Many children would appreciate the challenge of organizing a contest.

Happy Contesting!!

The American Kennel Club Junior Showmanship
The American Kennel Club
51 Madison Avenue
New York, NY 10010
For ages 10-18; kids enter their purebred dogs to be judged; contact your local AKC dog club for information or write to the above address; various ribbons or rosettes are prizes.

BOOK IT! National Reading Incentive Program
Pizza Hut, Inc.
P.O. Box 2905
Wichita, KS 67201
(800) 426-6548
bookit@pizzahut.com
For K-6 grades whose teachers decide to run BOOK IT! (homeschool groups welcome); teachers decide on the number of pages or books their students must read each month, if they reach their goal they receive certificates for free personal pan pizzas at Pizza Hut; if all the kids in your class (or homeschool group) complete each month successfully then your entire group can receive a pizza party from Pizza Hut at the end of the school year!

Child's Play Touring Theatre
2650 West Belden Avenue
Chicago, IL 60647
www.CPTT.com
For K-8 grades; this touring theatre performs plays, songs, and dances based on stories and poems written by children; when your group, school, organization, etc. invites them to come to your area, they ask children to submit their work; Child's Play judges the works and creates productions based on them. The children can then come and watch their stories come to life on the stage; seeing your story, poem, etc. performed and/or receiving a certificate from Child's Play are the prizes for this contest.

The Congressional Award
Congressional Award Foundation
P.O.Box 77440
Washington, DC 20013
(202) 226-0130
www.congressionalaward.org
The minimum age to register is 14 and you must achieve your goals by your 24th birthday;To earn this award you set goals in 4 areas: volunteer public service, personal development, physical fitness, and expedition/ exploration; you select an adult advisor to help you set your goals; the prize is a prestigious Congressional Award; 7000 awards have been given since 1979.

The DuPont Challenge Science Essay Awards Program
c/o General Learning Corporation
900 Skokie Blvd.
Suite 200
Northbrook, IL 60062
(847) 205-3000
For grades 7-12; a science writing competition; write an essay that describes a scientific development, challenge or event that has captured your interest; solid knowledge, research and creative, clear writing a must; cash prizes ranging from $50-$1500.

Freedoms Foundation's National Awards Program for Youth
Awards Department
Freedoms Foundation at Valley Forge
Route 23, P.O.Box 706
Valley Forge, PA 19482-0706
(610) 933-8825
For K-12 grades; write an essay about your efforts to be a responsible U.S. Citizen; may include scrapbook, photo album, etc. to substantiate your material; U.S. Savings Bonds and George Washington Honor Medals for prizes.

Kodak International Newspaper Snapshot Awards (KINSA)
This contest is cosponsored by Eastman Kodak Co. and participating newspapers across North America. Contact your local newspaper to see if they are participating. For all ages; amateur photographers only; prizes are on the local level and then International; International prizes are cash ranging from $50-$10,000!

LEGO Clubs
Lego Systems
555 Taylor Road
Enfield, CT 06083-1600
www.Lego.com
(860) 749-2291
Your child can enter contests found in the FREE MAGAZINE, *Mania Magazine*; various contests utilizing Legos; variety of prizes.

Make a Difference Day
USA Weekend/Make a Difference Day
1000 Wilson Blvd.
Arlington, VA 22229
MakeADifferenceDay.com
(703) 276-6445
All ages; a national day of volunteering held annually on the 4th Saturday in Oct.; do something good for your neighbor or community and write a description of what you did to *USA Weekend*; if you or your group are chosen as winners, donations will be given to a charity of your choice and you and your project will be featured in an issue of *USA Weekend*.

Math Olympiads
2154 Bellmore Avenue
Bellmore, NY 11710-5645
www.moems.org
moes@i-2000.com
Challenge your math students in grades 4 - 8! Homeschool teams haveparticipated and done very well in the Math Olympiads.
The Math Olympiads Program Purpose is:
To stimulate enthusiasm and a love for Mathematics
To introduce important Mathematical concepts
To teach major strategies for problem solving
To develop Mathematical flexibility in solving problems
To strengthen Mathematical intuition
To foster Mathematical creativity and ingenuity
To provide for the satisfaction, joy, and thrill of meeting challenges

Your homeschool's math club meets weekly for an hour. Club members explore a topic or strategy in depth, using Creative Problem Solving in School Mathematics (or other sources), or they practice for the contests, using nonroutine problems from Mathematical Olympiads Contest Problems for Elementary and Middle Schools (or other sources).

The highlights for students are the five monthly contests, given from November to March. No traveling is required. These contests provide an incentive for students to intensify their study of math.

Created in 1977 by Dr. George Lenchner, an internationally known math educator, the Math Olympiads went public in 1979. In 2000, 120,000 students from 5,000 teams worldwide participated in the Olympiads. All 50 states and 25 other countries were represented.

Choose from two grade appropriate divisions (4-6 and 7-8). For $85 per team ($125 foreign), the sponsor receives: All 25 problems and solutions from the previous year. New enrollees receive 50 problems and solutions from the previous two years. 5 contests: 35 copies of all questions and 1 copy of all solutions. 8 newsletters that lead the sponsor through all procedures, provide statistics and relevant information.Certificates for all students and awards for more than 50% of all participating students.

MATHCOUNTS
www.mathcounts.org
(703) 684-2828
mathcounts@nspe.org
MATHCOUNTS is the nationwide math coaching and competition program for middle school students. It promotes student interest in math by making math achievement as challenging, exciting and prestigious as a school sport. Beginning each fall, thousands of teachers, MATHCOUNTS alumni and other volunteers coach student mathletes using the free MATHCOUNTS School Handbook. After several months of coaching, registered schools select students to compete in one of 500 local competitions. The top teams and individuals then progress to state competitions, where the top four individuals advance to the National Competition. MATHCOUNTS is one of the country's largest and most successful education partnerships involving volunteers, educators, industry sponsors and students. Homeschoolers do participate in this!

National Geography Bee
National Geographic Society
National Geography Bee
1145 17th Street, NW
Washington, DC 20036-4688
www.national geographic.com/geographybee/index.html
Schools (and homeschool groups) with students in grades 4-8 may enter; school competitions begin with warm-up questions and then rounds of questions increasing in difficulty; register your school by writing to the above address; winners of your school may get to go to the state and then national levels; amongst other prizes, national winners receive college scholarships and large cash prizes.

Odyssey of the Mind Competitions
International Headquarters
Odyssey of Mind Program
c/o Creative Competitions, Inc.
1325 Rt. 130 South, Suite F
Gloucester City, NJ 08030
(856) 456-7776
info@odysseyofthemind.com
For ages 12 through collegiate; local, regional and world competitions; OM competition is a program that challenges kids to think creatively when presented with open-ended problems; team-work is important; judges look for unusual ideas and for style of presentation; medals and trophies are prizes.

P.A. Witty Outstanding Literature Award
Dr. Cathy Collins Block, Professor
School of Education
Box 297900
Texas Christain University
Fort Worth, TX 76129
(817) 257-7000
For elementary and secondary school students; send original poems, stories, or prose to this contest sponsored by the International Reading Assoc.; writing is judged on its creativity, originality, and beauty of expression; cash and certificates as prizes.

Pillsbury Bake-Off Contest
Pillsbury Company
2866 Pillsbury Center
Minneapolis, MN 55402-1464
(800) 767-4466
For ages 10 and up; share your favorite recipe and compete with other amateur cooks; recipes must use some Green Giant or Pillsbury product; Finalists receive expense paid trip to contest finals and grand winner receives big cash award.

Science Olympiad
5955 Little Pine Lane
Rochester Hills, MI 48306
(248) 651-4013
www.soinc.org
For grades 3-12, divided into age divisions; students solve scientific problems at local, state and national tournaments, either in teams or individually; the goal of the Science Olympiad is to encourage students and teachers to enjoy the challenges of science through teamwork and cooperation; winners receive medals and trophies.

Scripps Howard National Spelling Bee
312 Walnut Street
P.O. Box 5380
Cincinnati, OH 45201
http://spellingbee.com
bee@scripps.com
For grades 3-8; school, regional and then national finals; school participants receive medals and certificates; regional winners receive prizes and all expense paid trips to the National Spelling Bee in Washington, DC; National finalists share large cash prizes.

Also, your local chapters of **4-H and Boy Scouts/Girl Scouts of America** often sponsor contests in which your children may participate.

Appendix A: Resources
Correspondence/Umbrella Schools, and
On-Line Learning

A Beka Correspondence School
Box 18000
Pensacola, FL 32523-9160
(800) 874-2352
(Christian Pre-K through 12 traditional curriculum. Diploma option.)

Alpha Omega Academy Online
300 N. Mckemy Avenue
Chandler, AZ 85226-2618
(877) 688-2652 (Toll-free)
bola@switched-onschoolhouse.com
www.switched-onschoolhouse.com/aoao
(Christian. Uses Switched-On Schoolhouse multimedia curriculum.)

Calvert School
105 Tuscany Road
Baltimore, MD 21210
(410) 243-6030
(pre-K -8 Curriculum.)

Christian Liberty Academy Satellite Schools
502 West Euclid Ave.
Arlington Heights, IL 60004-5495
(800) 348-0899 (info packet)
(800) 832-2741 (catalog)
(Individualized curriculum with diploma option.)
www.homeschools.org

Clonlara School and Clonlara Compuhigh
1289 Jewitt St.
Ann Arbor, MI 48104
(734) 769-4511
www.clonlara.org

Covenant Home Curriculum
Stonewood Village
17700 W. Capitol Drive
Brookfield, WI 53045
(262) 781-2171
(Classical Christian curriculum.)

Escondido Tutorial Service (ETS)
2634 Bernardo Avenue
Escondido, CA 92029
(760) 746-0980
www.gbt.org

Escondido Tutorial Service is "dedicated to bringing classical Christian education to homeschoolers." Tutorials are available through the Internet. Examples of ETS courses: Great Books Tutorial: This 6 year survey of Western Literature will guide your child through the books that have shaped our cultural historical. Constitutional Law with Michael Farris: Study under one of our finest Christian constitutional lawyers. Saxon Tutorials: Algebra I, Algebra 2, Advanced Mathematics and Physics. Logic: Learn rules that govern correct thinking. Shakespeare: Takes your child through the plays of the Great Bard. We've been pleased with the quality instruction.

Hewitt Homeschooling Resources
2103 B Street, PO Box 9
Washougal, WA 98671
(360) 835-8708
www.hewitthomeschooling.com
(Curriculum for both special needs & high achievers.)

Home Study International
PO Box 4437
Silver Spring, MD 20914-4437
(800) 782-GROW
(Secular & Seventh Day Adventist materials.)

Indiana University High School
(800) 334-1011
extend@indiana.edu
http://scsindiana.edu
"Earn your high school diploma through distance education."

Keystone National High School
School House Station
420 West 5th Street
Bloomsburg, PA 17815-1564
(800) 255-4937
info@keystonehighschool.com
www.keystonehighschool.com
(Accredited, secular correspondence school.)

PA Homeschoolers
Pennsylvania Homeschoolers
RR 2 Box 117
Kittanning, PA 16201
(412) 783-6512
www.pahomeschoolers.com
(On-line classes and more.)

Seton Home Study School
1350 Progress Drive
Front Royal, VA 22630
(540) 636-9990
(K-12 traditional Catholic program.)

University of Nebraska-Lincoln
Clifford Hardin Nebraska Center for Continuing Education
PO Box 839100
Lincoln, NE 68583-9100
(402) 472-2175
www.unl.edu/unlpub/index.shtml

The Westbridge Academy
1610 West Highland Avenue #228
Chicago, IL 60660
(773) 743-3312
www.westbridgeacademy.com
(This umbrella school is especially designed for gifted
and highly motivated homeschoolers. Classical and individually-planned
education.)

Curriculum Resources

The Annenburg Press
(800) LEARNER
Ask for the catalog.
They supply the tapes for The Mechanical Universe (AP physics course)

Bright Ideas Press
PO Box 333
Cheswold, DE 19936
(877) 492-8081
www.BrightIdeasPress.com
Hogan@BrightIdeasPress.com
Maggie and Bob Hogan's company produces and sells a variety of curriculum and resources for your bright student.

Castle Heights Press, Inc.
106 Caldwell Drive
Baytown, TX 77520
(800) 763-7148
http://www.flash.net/~wx3o/chp
Julicher@aol.com
Kathleen Julicher's company. Science lab materials, manuals, and unit studies. Grades K -12. Materials very appropriate for gifted students.

Christian Home Educators Press
12440 Firestone Blvd.
Suite 1008
Norwalk, CA 90650
The High School Handbook: Junior and Senior High School at Home
by Mary Schofield. $19.97. This is an excellent book to walk you through the process. Well organized and bursting with information!

Critical Thinking Press
P.O. Box 448
Pacific Grove, CA 93950
(800) 458-48
www.criticalthinking.com

Education +Plus
PO Box 1350
Taylors, SC 29687
(864) 609-5411
info@edplus.com
www.edplus.com
Inge and Ronald Cannon's company is committed to helping parents train their children for God's glory. Many wonderful resources including Inge Cannon's exceptional work on mentoring teens and apprenticeship. If you've ever had the opportunity to sit under Inge's dynamic teaching at a homeschool seminar, you know you're in for a real treat in her catalog.

Greater Testing Concepts
The Art of Problem Solving
P.O. Box A-D
Stanford, CA 94309

Home School Resource Center
1425 E. Chocolate Ave.
Hershey, PA 17033
(717) 533-1669
www.debrabell.com
Call for their catalog - it's a gem!

Home Training Tools
2827 Buffalo Horn Dr.
Laurel, MT 59044-8325
(800) 860-6272
Fax: (888) 860-2344
email: homett@mcn.net
www.hometrainingtools.com
Great science resources.

The Teaching Company
7405 Alban Station Court
Suite A-107
Springfield, VA 22150
(800) 832-2412
www.teachco.com
Secular high school and college level courses on audio and video tape with workbooks. The Los Angeles Times says, "Passionate, erudite, living legend lecturers...Academia's best lecturers are being captured on tape."

Teacher Ideas Press
Libraries Unlimited
P.O. Box 6633
Englewood, CO 80155-6633
(800) 237-6124
www.lu.com

Timberdoodle Co.
1510 E. Spencer Lk Road
Shelton, WA 98584
(360) 426-0672
www.timberdoodle.com
Interesting assortment of practical, wholesome curriculum, educational toys,
and materials. Get your Fishertechnik™ Kits here.

Appendix B:
Magazines and Organizations for the Gifted

The College Guide for Academically Talented Students
Duke University TIP
Box 90747
Durham, NC 27708
(919) 684-3847
www.tip.duke.edu/

Gifted Child Quarterly
Periodical of more scholarly papers.
also
Parenting for High Potential
A magazine for parents and children.
National Association for Gifted Children
1707 L Street NW, Suite 550
Washington DC 20036
(202) 785-4268
www.nagc.org

Gifted Child Today Magazine
A resource for nurturing talented children.
Prufrock Press
P.O. Box 8813
Waco, TX 76714-8813
(800) 998-2208

Gifted Resources Home Page
www.eskimo.com/~user/kids.html

Imagine...Opportunities and Resources for Academically Talented Youth
Johns Hopkins University
(800) 548-1784

Understanding Our Gifted
Dedicated to helping gifted children reach their full potential.
P.O. Box 18268
Boulder, CO 80308-8268
$30.00 per year (6 issues)

Appendix C:
Guides to Distance Learning &
College Information

The Electronic University, a Guide to Distant Learning Programs
Peterson's Guides, Inc.
Princeton, New Jersey

The Christian Connector
(800) 667-0600
A **free** resource pack for students interested in attending Christian colleges.

Goshen Internet Christian Resource Directory to Christian Colleges and Universities
www.goshen.net

Peterson's On-line College & Careers Center
www.petersons.com

Princeton Review Website
www.reveiw.com

National Association of Student Financial Aid Administrators.
Free information and links to financial aid resources including FastWEB.
www.finaid.org

Web sites worth a visit:

www.whatsthebest-college.com
Christian college online search by categories.

www.homeschoolteenscollege.net

www.christiancolleges.com

Projected Course Sequence

Now   Year [   ]   Grade [   ]   Year [   ]

Grade [   ]   Year [   ]   Grade [   ]   Year [   ]

Grade [   ]   Year [   ]   Grade [   ]   Year [   ]

Chapter Compacting Planner

Subject _____

Objectives or main ideas in Chapter (s) _____	Reinforcement Activities (if necessary) (worksheet pages, review questions, activity sheets, vocabulary, exercises, problem sets)	Mastered: how demonstrated / date
1.		
2.		
3.		
4.		
5.		
6.		

Scheduling

Prior time to complete _____

Planned time to complete _____

Lesson Numbers (correspond to hour)	Course Compacting Planner	Subject	Time
1.	40.	79.	118.
2.	41.	80.	119.
3.	42.	81.	120.
4.	43.	82.	121.
5.	44.	83.	122.
6.	45.	84.	123.
7.	46.	85.	124.
8.	47.	86.	125.
9.	48.	87.	126.
10.	49.	88.	127.
11.	50.	89.	128.
12.	51.	90.	129.
13.	52.	91.	130.
14.	53.	92.	131.
15.	54.	93.	132.
16.	55.	94.	133.
17.	56.	95.	134.
18.	57.	96.	135.
19.	58.	97.	136.
20.	59.	98.	137.
21.	60.	99.	138.
22.	61.	100.	139.
23.	62.	101.	140.
24.	63.	102.	141.
25.	64.	103.	142.
26.	65.	104.	143.
27.	66.	105.	144.
28.	67.	106.	145.
29.	68.	107.	146.
30.	69.	108.	147.
31.	70.	109.	148.
32.	71.	110.	149.
33.	72.	111.	150.
34.	73.	112.	
35.	74.	113.	
36.	75.	114.	Basis: 150 hours
37.	76.	115.	_____ Chapters
38.	77.	116.	_____ Labs
39.	78.	117.	_____ Field trips
			_____ Days

Independent Project/Study Planner

Name of course
for credit _____

Research Needed
   Activities Planned
      Product / Result
	Resources
	needed
		Hours
		required

Total hours spent		

Advisor(s) / sponsor(s)
    business/ address / phone / email address

Community Service Record

Organisation Address Phone Supervisor	Job Description	Dates worked	Hours worked

Activity / Honors / Awards Record

Organisation Address Phone Supervisor	Position held (dates of office)	Award or honor (date awarded)	Dates of membership	Projects accomplished

Secondary School Record

Name _____

Birthdate _____

Date of Graduation _____

Courses	Level (Honors, Advanced Placement, Regular)	First Course				Credit earned	Second Course				Credit earned
		1	2	3	4		1	2	3	4	
Spiritual Training											
English Language											
Math											
Science											
Social Studies											
Fine Arts											
Foreign Languages											
Other											

For personal file: copy onto cardstock for permanent record.

High School Transcript

Grading Scale
A
B
C
D
F

Name _____ Gender _____

Birthdate _____ School code _____

Address_____ Telephone _____

Fax _____ e-mail _____

City_____ State _____ Zip _____

Additional notes, awards, and
enrollment data on reverse side

Date of Graduation _____ GPA (high school) _____ Total Credits (high school) _____

Courses	Grade	Credit(s)	Courses	Grade	Credit(s)
_____	_____	_____	_____	_____	_____
_____	_____	_____	_____	_____	_____
_____	_____	_____	_____	_____	_____
_____	_____	_____	_____	_____	_____
_____	_____	_____	_____	_____	_____
_____	_____	_____	_____	_____	_____
_____	_____	_____	_____	_____	_____
_____	_____	_____	_____	_____	_____
_____	_____	_____	_____	_____	_____
_____	_____	_____	_____	_____	_____
_____	_____	_____	_____	_____	_____
_____	_____	_____	_____	_____	_____
_____	_____	_____	_____	_____	_____
_____	_____	_____	_____	_____	_____
_____	_____	_____	_____	_____	_____
_____	_____	_____	_____	_____	_____
_____	_____	_____	_____	_____	_____

PSAT SI_____

  Date:_____ Age: ____

    Math_____

    Verbal _____

    Writing _____

ACT

  Date:_____ Age:_____

    English _____

    Math _____

    Reading _____

    Science _____

    Composite _____

SAT II test	Score	Date
_____		
_____		
_____		
_____		

AP test	Score	Date
_____		
_____		

SAT

  Date: _____ Age: _____

    Math _____

    Verbal _____

    Writing _____

Attendance*

	Year 1	Year 2	Year 3	Year 4
Present				
Absent				

*may not be required

Castle Heights Press

SCIENCE LAB
at
HOME

Experiences in Biology $ 24.95
An assortment of experiments which match your equipment and interests. Teaches foundational principles of biology. Answers.

Experiences in Chemistry $24.95
EASY experiments which integrate with any high school chemistry text.

Experiences in Physics : High school physics laboratory manual. New! Modern! Wonderful questions. Answers $24.95

Student Databooks for each manual above $9.95

More excellent resources!!
The Junior Scientist's Field Journal: A special place to record and draw those special observations. $9.95

The Herbarium: Keep your leaves and botanical samples. $9.95

Geometric Constructions Interesting scenarios/problems which require use of geometric construction methods. $9.95

The Ultimate Science Project Notebook Science Fair help on presenting and 50 ideas for uncommon projects. $9.95

Project-Oriented Science: A Teacher's Guide $14.95
A guide for planning an elementary science class using text, experiments, and skill-building. Includes masters.

Hands-on Science: Hundreds of experiments for the 2nd-6th grade student. Principles of particles in motion and how they affect weather, thermodynamics, and aviation. $24.95

Gifted Children at Home: A wonderful resource for families with gifted children. Curriculum hints, identification of giftedness, and much, much more. $24.95

Unit Studies & More ($ 9.95 each)

One Week Off: Horses: Study on horses and horseback riding.

One Week Off: Aviation: Unit study on aviation & flying.

One Week Off: Space Exploration: Study space travel.

One Week Off: Like a Shepherd: Sheep, their upkeep, structure, and wool. Discover how we are like sheep.

One Week Off: Dogs & Puppies: Dogs: domesticated and wild.

One Week Off: Cats & Kittens: Cats: house, barn, and wild cats.

One Week Off: Drama: The theater, plays, characters, types of drama from comedies to melodrama.

One Week Off: Cars: Unit study on cars. Ideal for your young driver.

My First Unit Study: Horses Let your young student study about horses along with her older brother or sister. A unit study made for younger children.

My First Science Notebook Science skills for the youngest science students.

My Science Notebook 2 Follows My First Science Notebook

Cooking & Science: Classic experiments using classic recipes: Secondary level difficulty. A great way to do chemistry laboratory.

Cooking & Science for Elementary Students
Real science in the kitchen doing real science. $ 9.95

Homeschool Assignment Notebook $ 7.95
Record keeping for the homeschooled student. Dated and organised for easy recordkeeping.

Pathways in Science:
A popular worktext covering introductory physical science: chemistry, physics, aviation, geology, space science, and rocketry. Written from a Christian perspective, this book has labs, chapter reviews, and vocabulary exercises. Tests & answers included. $34.95

Order Form

Ship To: _____

_____

_____

Phone number: _____

Credit Card orders (Visa/Mastercard/Discover accepted)
Card Number   Expiration date

Signature

Castle Heights Press, Inc.
106 Caldwell Drive
Baytown, TX 77520
1-800-763-7148
Julicher@aol.com
http://www.castleheightspress.com

Quantity	Title	Price Each	Extended Price
	Subtotal		
	Tax (8.0%)		
	S&H $5.50 minimum or 15%		
	Total		

BRIGHT IDEAS PRESS
ORDER FORM
www.BrightIdeasPress.com

Mail your check or money order to:
Bright Ideas Press
P.O. Box 333
Cheswold, DE 19936
Toll Free: 877.492.8081

VISA & MasterCard orders are accepted. See below for information.

Prices Good Through
Until March 31, 2002
SHIPPING TABLE
Up to $50……..………$6.00
$51 - $150………….….10%
over $150……………….free
Most orders are shipped within 3 business days. Please allow 3-4 weeks from May-July.

Item #	Description	Qty.	Price	Amount
GC-100	The Ultimate Geography & Timeline Guide		34.95	
BIP-1	Hands-On Geography		14.95	
BIP-2	The Scientist's Apprentice		26.95	
BIP-3	Student History Notebook of America		12.95	
BIP-4	Over Our Heads In Wonder		9.95	
GG-102	Gifted Children At Home		24.95	
SCIAP-1	The Scientist's Apprentice Package w/ 9 reading plan books		75.00	
DW-YR1	Diana Waring Year 1 Package–Ancient Civilization		60.00	

SHIP TO ADDRESS: Please PRINT clearly

Name: _____

Address: _____

_____

Phone: ( ) _____

Email: _____

Special!
FREE SHIPPING
*on *orders* over $150.00*

Sub Total	
⇐ **Shipping Cost:** See Shipping Table	
Total Amount Due	$

Credit Card Information

_____

VISA/MasterCard Number   Exp. Date

_____

Signature